Technical politics

MANCHESTER
1824

Manchester University Press

Technical politics

Andrew Feenberg's critical
theory of technology

Graeme Kirkpatrick

Manchester University Press

Published by Manchester University Press
Altrincham Street, Manchester M1 7JA
www.manchesteruniversitypress.co.uk

British Library Cataloguing-in-Publication Data
A catalogue record for this book is available from the British Library

ISBN 978 1 5261 0532 5 hardback
ISBN 978 1 5261 0534 9 open access

First published 2020

The publisher has no responsibility for the persistence or accuracy of URLs for any external or third-party internet websites referred to in this book, and does not guarantee that any content on such websites is, or will remain, accurate or appropriate.

Typeset by Newgen Publishing UK

Contents

Acknowledgements

I could not have written this book without the assistance of many people, principal among them Andrew Feenberg, who, ever since I first turned up on his doorstep in 2002, clutching an apple tart from one of the bakeries near his apartment in Paris, has been unstintingly generous with his time and unbelievably patient when listening to my criticisms of his ideas. We haven't always agreed on the finer points of critical theory and technology but of his kindness there has never been any doubt. I will have succeeded if, based on our conversations, this book clarifies some of his arguments, or persuades more readers of the relevance of his intervention. On points where he and I disagree, I hope to have provided material for further discussion that might itself clarify and develop the critical theory of technology.

Parts of some chapters have been presented as papers to different audiences, who have made comments and suggestions that helped me reach the version presented here. Chapter 2, on formal bias, benefited from a critical discussion with Yoni Van Den Eede and participants at the 'Technology, Society, Change' symposium he organised at the Vrije Universiteit Brussel in Summer 2011, and I am grateful to them. Chapter 1 was the basis of a sociology seminar in the University of Manchester in spring 2017, attended by several colleagues in the sociology department and some people from elsewhere in the university. In summer 2019, I presented parts of Chapter 5 at the annual conference of the Utopian Studies Society in Prato, where the comments and questions received helped me when it came to writing the final draft. I'd like to thank everyone who participated in these events. I'd also like to record my appreciation of the students on my undergraduate course, Technology & Society, which ran at Manchester from 2007 to 2014 and included many fascinating discussions of Feenberg's work, often initiated by their criticisms and suggestions.

It is increasingly difficult in the modern university to find time for one's own ideas, still less anyone else's, so it is humbling when people read or discuss your project and think about it enough to enthuse, disagree, or point out things you missed. The following people have been generous in this way with their time, ideas and encouragement, so I am grateful to them: Alice Bloch, Lars Brondum, Bridget Byrne, Alan Carling, Colin Craig, Garry Crawford, Nick Crossley, Simin Fadaee, Susan Halford, Steve Hall, Helen Kennedy, Lars Kristensen, Clive Lawson, Cheryl Martens, Peter McMylor, Nadim Mirshak, Angela Ndalianis, Richie Nimmo, Cristiana Olcese, Tom Redshaw, Nick Thoburn and Feng Zhu.

For their extraordinary patience and constant support for the project I'd also like to thank Caroline Wintersgill, who suggested that I write this book in the first place, and Alun Richards at Manchester University Press. An anonymous reviewer for MUP made a number of useful suggestions and I'm grateful to them as well. All remaining faults with the work are, of course, my own responsibility.

My greatest thanks are to Sarah Carling for her support, encouragement and unfailing intellectual curiosity.

Introduction: from critical theory to technical politics

Technical politics is the name for disputes over technology design involving social actors with different values, interests and ideas about the future shape of society. Such disputes are surely as old as technology itself but in the modern, industrial period they tended to involve quite narrow sections of society, and the resultant technology served very specific economic interests. In the digital era, this has changed as people everywhere are shaping and customising devices and networks to suit their own preferences. The new era of popular interventions in technical practice creates openings for progressive politics, in which values other than the narrow pursuit of profit might shape technical infrastructure. At the same time, the objective need for new technologies, to address climate change and other imminent catastrophes, has never been more obvious or urgent.

This book is a critical study of the work of Andrew Feenberg, philosopher of technology and exponent of a unique version of critical theory. Grounded in the tradition of Marx and the Frankfurt School, Feenberg's project is political and avowedly left-wing, even socialist in orientation. His work is distinguished from other versions of critical theory by its basically optimistic assessment of the role of technology in social change. Feenberg's concept of technical politics attempts to mediate between the democratisation of technical practices on one hand, and the need for civilisational change to move humanity onto a sustainable footing on the other.

In this version of critical theory, technology retains the progressive role assigned to it by Marx – one that had receded to the horizon, or even been reversed in the work of earlier generations of critical theorists, who associated it with instrumental reason and the disenchantment of the world. Strangely enough, Feenberg also retains some of these negative ideas but incorporates them into an understanding of technology that

1

grasps it in terms of its fundamental ambivalence. He presents a definition of technology that is both conceptually nuanced and at the same time sensitive to historical variation in a way that distinguishes his work and sets it above even the most sophisticated positions in contemporary philosophy of technology.[1]

This work of conceptualisation is inseparable from Feenberg's conviction that technology is profoundly political and, moreover, that the principal political challenge faced by humanity today concerns its technology. In trying to establish the truth about what technology is, Feenberg at the same time elaborates a thesis on the politics of its place in cultural modernity. This involves the claim that technological change is not merely a driver of modernisation, and neither is it a factor that impedes or delimits the scope of politics and the pursuit of enlightened or progressive social reforms. In disclosing the 'historical essence' of technology Feenberg reveals that it is the very medium of political transformation: that activity conducted in the technical sphere, informed by extra-technical discursive factors, is the locus of political potential in modern societies. In short, he identifies technology as the site of political praxis: *technical politics*.

The idea of technical politics, then, combines Marx's enthusiasm for technology as the driver of social change and political progress with critical theory's suspicion of technology as the locus of societal rationalisation. Feenberg achieves this by locating both sides of this contradiction, so to speak, as internal to his account of what technology is, so that it is itself a constitutively contradictory phenomenon, while at the same time demonstrating that technology is always socially contested. Indeed, Feenberg goes so far as to say that technology is the distinctive form taken by politics today. His work speaks directly to the concerns of those who advocate technological acceleration as the route out of our contemporary crisis. Nick Srnicek and Alex Williams (2017), for example, converge with Feenberg in seeking to reclaim the project of modernity and, like him, they take reflection on technology's potential as a kind of licence to 'think big' about the prospects for future civilisation. However, their analysis lacks any account of how the willed transformation of technology they seek is to be brought about, so they can only genuflect to the need for new networks of institutions, presumably brought into existence by the (not inconsiderable) force of their polemic. In contrast, Feenberg takes what they dismiss as 'folk' interventions in technology as a starting point but adds a strategic theorisation of the technical as political, and in so doing provides essential conceptual resources with which to move from wish fulfilment to tactical analysis.

Feenberg's project is a synthesis of many currents of thought, and it introduces several important concepts that arise from this. Like any theory of such scale and ambition, his runs the risk of eclecticism, in which disparate concepts and sources are forced together despite not really being compatible. One of the tasks of a book like the present one, which is part exposition and exegesis but also part critique, is to pull apart what has been carefully sewn together in order to give the reader a vantage point from which to judge the success of the larger project for themselves. It behoves the author of such a work to acknowledge that the putting together was much more difficult than the pulling apart. The conscience of said author is partly allayed by the fact that pulling at threads of this quality is very enjoyable and that the activity is a kind of compliment to the intelligence that wove them together.

The first duty of a book like this, though, is to try and convey a sense of the value and importance of the work that is being discussed. Why does Feenberg write about technology, and what is he trying to tell us about it? Why does he tell us that Heidegger's insights are important and worth hanging onto, while at the same time demonstrating the depth and extent of error in the philosophy that gave rise to them? How can he draw on Foucault's critique of the human sciences and also defend an idea of progressive technological rationalisation? Why does he condemn the Frankfurt School as miserabilists who often fail to deliver on their own promises, while calling his own theory the 'critical theory of technology'? Is Feenberg some (any) kind of Marxist, or is he a utopian socialist? These questions, and others concerning the details of his system, are all addressed in this book, but first it is necessary to position his intervention in contemporary thought about technology and society.

My contention is that Feenberg's primary focus has been the development of a theory of technology as something that is always already political. What he calls 'technical politics' is the central concept around which the rest of his system falls into place and in light of which its various points of obscurity and difficulty may best be clarified and understood. In this introduction I will attempt to situate it historically and theoretically, as well as providing an overview of the current book and describing the basis of my own critical perspective.

1 Critical theory in context

Feenberg began publishing on technology in the early 1990s, prior to which he published a study of Georg Lukàcs and the young Marx (Feenberg 1981). His interest in technology, however, pre-dates the published work and must have been present in his relationship with Herbert Marcuse, who supervised Feenberg's doctoral studies in the 1960s and early 1970s. This relationship is surely the most important and influential one on the development of Feenberg's thought, and it is fair to say that he has done more than any other thinker to update and extend Marcuse's theory, to give it contemporary relevance.

A key moment in Feenberg's intellectual formation was his involvement in the 1968 events in Paris. There is a photograph of him outside the gates of the Renault factory where students and workers famously came together in a bid to wrest social power from the capitalist class and their political representatives.[2] As documented in his co-authored book about those events (Feenberg and Freedman 2001), this bid was partly successful. For a few weeks the power of the government of Charles de Gaulle was undermined and the president fled the country. In Paris and elsewhere in France basic social functions like the distribution of food were taken over by informal networks of people motivated to create an alternative social system.

In common with others of his generation who participated in the May events, Feenberg has a special light in his eyes when they are discussed, and it would not be an exaggeration to say that *les événements* have the status of an article of faith for him. As is widely noted in the commentary on 1968, many of the people involved were profoundly affected by something they experienced then. The near religious character of the May events is evidenced by the way that disputes over their interpretation quickly involve accusations of betrayal. Among those, like Alain Badiou, Jacques Rancière and indeed Feenberg, who retain their conviction that willed, wholesale changes of social system in wealthy countries remain possible and desirable, 1968 stands as confirmation. As such, their collective memory is an ideological bulwark against cynicism and nihilism, both of which serve as gateway drugs to political apathy and capitulation.

This has a profound bearing on the mature thought of the philosophers of the class of '68. Feenberg's theory is informed by his enduring conviction that capitalist modernity is susceptible to radical, even revolutionary transformation. Like Rancière (2009), his understanding of this assigns a specific role to aesthetics and to the changing role of the human senses in history. For both these thinkers, as for the young Marx, the senses are shaped and reconfigured by social and cultural contexts that promote the need for sharpened perception in some circumstances while dulling it in others. Capitalism produces a sensory configuration attuned to a world based on equivalences and exchange, while socialist perception would be more diverse, offering access to a fuller, more sensuous kind of experience. Like Marcuse, Feenberg retrieves this idea from Marx's 1844 *Manuscripts* (Marx 1983), and deploys it as part of his account of the nature of technology under capitalism and the politics of technological transformation.

Marcuse famously visited Paris during the 1968 uprising and addressed meetings of the students and workers. For him, the upheavals of the time must have been a kind of vindication. In *Eros and Civilization* (1961) and *One-Dimensional Man* (1964) he had speculated that the totally rationalised, sexually repressed societies of Western civilisation had a chink in their armour. Educated youth, especially those groomed for a role in the technical professions, might refuse to take the places assigned to them. Their possession of technical skills and knowledge could, paradoxically enough, lead them to develop the possibility not of a less rationalised social system but of one in which rationality was developed to a new level, restored to the role set for it by the Enlightenment of improving human life rather than merely engineering the superficial 'happiness' of the satisfied consumer.

Marcuse's positive response to the 1960s student uprisings was in marked contrast to the attitudes of other members of his generation of critical theorists. His contemporaries, the Frankfurt School theorists Max Horkheimer and Theodor Adorno, reacted to student demonstrations and occupations in Germany with fear and suspicion. Indeed, excessive caution seems to have marked their attitude to any direct political engagement.[3] Adorno is said to have been troubled to find that his ideas might have inspired any kind of spontaneous social movements and considered that this was based on a misunderstanding. That was not unreasonable, given his negative assessment of the redemptive powers of political discourse. Horkheimer's revulsion at the behaviour of the students was such that he ended up expressing support for the US war in Vietnam.[4] It is not difficult to see why, for Feenberg and other students of the 1960s, Marcuse was a more appealing figure.

At the heart of the difference between these two versions of critical theory is a disagreement over psychoanalysis and what it has to tell Marxist theory about the nature of capitalist societies and the prospects for revolution. According to Marcuse's reading of Freud, consumerism enabled capitalism to move from straightforward, nineteenth-century repression of sexual instincts to a managed process whereby desires that might be destabilising to social order were re-cathected to the commodity, effectively channelling the basic drives into forms of consumption. Gratification was achieved through the cultivation of false needs and the endless deferral of real satisfaction into the behaviour patterns of acquisitive individualism. The way out of this, led by a generation of progressive technocrats, lay in the recovery of natural embodied desires and demand for the satisfaction of real needs, which consumer capitalism could not provide. There is a direct connection between these theoretical views and the radical cultural politics of the students, which involved ideas like flower power, free love and sexual liberation (Neville 1971).

Adorno's view was more austere and based on a different kind of refusal. Perhaps reflecting the mark made on him by the catastrophic events of the mid-twentieth century, he feared any project that might unleash the darker forces of the id. Like Marcuse, he worked out of the problematic that seeks reconciliation of subject and object, and for him too this involved a dimension that could only be adequately explored using the psychoanalytic concepts of desire and repression. He also described the culture industry in terms of false needs and misdirected desire. However, for him, the notion of real needs was more obscure, and identifying it with the liberation of desire in a kind of somatic condition of bliss was a false route, likely to lead nowhere or to somewhere even worse than consumerism.

As Espen Hamer (2005) points out, Adorno proposed a different understanding of the subjective dynamics of life under capitalism, in which liberation is modelled more closely on the struggle for a kind of Kantian autonomy, albeit one that is informed by a richer portrayal of psychic life than was available to eighteenth-century philosophy. The political implications of his approach are correspondingly less clear than those of Marcuse's and probably more conservative.

Critical theory in Europe has moved on since Adorno and Marcuse, and second- and third-generation Frankfurt theorists have repudiated their forebears on a number of important points. Of obvious importance here is the work of Jürgen Habermas,[5] who has penned important critiques of both Adorno and Marcuse, and who has developed a very different version of critical theory based on theoretical foundations that have more in common with pragmatism than with the Marxist dialectic. His work also draws more heavily on ideas from development psychology than on psychoanalysis. Habermas is a few years older than Feenberg, and his work has framed the contemporary understanding of what Frankfurt School-inspired critical theory is in the twenty-first century. It is therefore worth itemising, albeit quite schematically, the major points of difference between his work and that of earlier critical theory, in order to place Feenberg's contribution in this context.

First, Habermas (1990) claims that what he calls the philosophy of consciousness has been superseded by the philosophy of language. Assimilating insights from Wittgenstein and pragmatism, Habermas moves critical theory into a theoretical context dominated by the study of language. This has a bearing on all aspects of his work. Ethics, for example, is less a matter of seeking internal coherence for a subject whose actions should be in line with privately processed maxims of conduct, and becomes instead a matter of consistency with norms integral to structures embedded in speech and verbal communication. Habermas considers that interpersonal efforts of communication are premised on a founding orientation to consensus and that this imposes ethical constraints on social actors. This focus on communication leads him to distinguish analytically between contexts of action, depending on the kind and extent of communicative orientation they imply. The development of a cultural lifeworld based on meaning is then distinguishable from the evolution of a systems sphere in which technical imperatives routinely determine what is done, without communicative deliberation. This pragmatic delineation of action domains gives a functional-evolutionary conception of the social formation, which supersedes historical materialism (1985). On this basis Habermas rejects the key critical notions of historicism and totality. His model of society is autonomous in its key features from any historical considerations, and its two dimensions interlock on the basis of a sociological functionalism that posits no overall direction for societal or historical development (1989).

Habermas's theory is 'critical' only in the fairly minimal sense that by clarifying the fundamental properties of the cultural lifeworld as ruled by norms implicit in communication, he succeeds in identifying the main threat to meaning in contemporary society through the idea of 'internal colonisation' (1985). The latter involves a corruption or distortion of communicative processes so that practices which ought to be mediated through speech and discussion aimed at reaching agreement are instead 'steered' by money or power. The latter are systems media that can 'reach through' communicative acts to impose an alien logic on events in the cultural lifeworld. The practical thrust of this theory lies in the direction of containment of the systems sphere, which, through colonisation, poses the permanent threat of becoming overweening and eliminating the positive role of shared meanings as a factor in the mediation of collective life.

Feenberg's theory incorporates ideas from Marcuse and first-generation Frankfurt theorists, but he combines them with an emphasis on communication that is, at times, quite Habermasian. He does not, however, completely repudiate the philosophy of consciousness, since, as we shall see, he retains an important role for both aesthetics and phenomenological analysis of ideas, specifically those operative at the scene of technology design, in his account of technology's alignment with social power and in his understanding of the politics of socio-technical change. Similarly, Feenberg retains an idea of the historical totality as a quasi-organic entity with its own dialectical developmental principles. His theory of technical politics is underpinned by the belief that more democracy in technology design will issue in a more humane society, culminating in what he calls 'civilizational change'. Moreover, while Habermas embraces pragmatism as a philosophy, with attendant limitations on what counts as real for social *science*, Feenberg retains from earlier critical theorists the notion of a wider reality that exceeds contemporary science and even plays an important role in social and historical change.

In all these ways, Feenberg is a traditional critical theorist who refuses the Habermasian update. At the same time, he introduces innovations of his own to Marcusean critical theory, also based on subsequent philosophical developments. In particular, Feenberg does not accept the consignment of technology to a separate, systems sphere beyond the scope of theories of social and cultural meaning. Technology, he argues, can be more or less meaningful depending on its social and historical location. One of his key innovations is to insist that both communication and the drive to create efficient and effective connections that characterise Habermas's systems dimension are best understood as combined *inside* the technical sphere. This is a subtle introjection of the central opposition of Habermasian theory, and it has important consequences.

2 Digital technology and critique

Feenberg's thesis that technology is essentially historical and ambivalent was formulated under its own very specific historical and cultural conditions. The argument that technology – its design and use – are not merely political but actually constitutive of contemporary politics is plausible because it coincides with the rise of digital technology and culture. Since the 1990s in particular, much of what was formerly understood as social activity, involving embodied actors in real-world places, has moved online. In this sense, the principal forums of social activism and debate about political issues are more highly mediatised than ever before. The rise of mass internet use, followed by the ongoing absorption of much of society into social media, has its origins in the same counter-cultural context that gave rise to the 1968 revolts.

Personal or home computer technology was first propounded in the mid-1970s and swiftly found a place for itself in the liberal ethos of the US West Coast (Freiberger and Swain 1984). The first such computers were shaped by a counter-culture that identified them as tools for self-emancipation and for the revival of democracy and community, in opposition to consumer culture and 'the system'. This culture had a strong 'do-it-yourself', craft ethos and was motivated by the search for social connection and authenticity. To an extent it was anti-technological, yet it included sub-groups for whom specific kinds of technology were viewed positively as tools of liberation. In this cultural setting the notion of a small computer had appeal because it presented the opportunity to take computer power from the system and give it to the people. Computer clubs and hobbyist groups sprang up to embrace the new machines, with slogans like 'computer power to the people' (Levy 1984). In his study of the social currents that shaped home computing, Fred Turner (2006) describes how counter-cultural icon Richard Brand's 'Whole Earth' movement combined a 'back to nature' ethos with the idea of using computers to connect people who shared the same alternative values and facilitate their activities.

This social context informed the design culture of computing and, in the course of the 1980s and 1990s, affected the way that computers were presented to the wider public. Within the emergent discipline of human–computer interface design the dominant trend was to create machines that did not seem or feel like machines and which interacted with humans through more or less 'natural' communicative processes. Austere command lines gave way to sumptuous graphical user interfaces, and computing culture became 'post-modern' (Turkle 1995) as it based human interaction with computers on simulation and play rather than the acquisition of technical knowledge. This tendency towards pleasurable computing developed in tandem with the popularisation of the Internet in the 1990s, itself made possible by the development of the world wide web and 'user-friendly', graphically enabled web browsing. A key value of the counter-culture had been play rather than work, and this was reflected in the emergence of online social spaces that included fantasy worlds and massive multi-player gaming environments. By the turn of the century the counter-culture may have passed away, but many of its values had been parsed into design principles of the digital revolution (Kirkpatrick 2013).

Key among those values was the notion of democratic participation. This was present in the aspirations of the early hobbyists and foregrounded again in the rhetorics of 'Web 2.0' in the first decade of this century. The meaning of technology has been transformed by this principle. In the industrial epoch technology consisted of machines that people were obliged to use as part of their work. Machines were progressive in the sense that they enhanced productive efficiency, but few people were keen to work with one. To be sure, there were gadgets for the home and some dedicated devices for leisure use, but in recent decades technology has become as strongly associated with leisure as it is with labour. Connection to the Internet via a smartphone is almost a necessary condition for social participation, and this is experienced not as an imposition of the system but as a portal to opportunities for play, social connection and enjoyment. Technology has crossed some kind of line, and it has been pushed by the actions of millions of individuals driving its design and its acquisition of functions.

This change is vital to Feenberg's project because the fact of popular involvement in technology design constitutes the definitive opening to technical politics. His point is not merely that technology design is political because it conditions all of this activity. It is also not simply that nearly all social interaction is now mediatised and so political activity requires some kind of technological knowledge. For Feenberg, the fact that people consciously shape technology is the form taken by contemporary politics. In much the same way that Badiou (2006) dismisses most of what passes for politics in contemporary society as an empty exchange of well-rehearsed platitudes that changes nothing, so Feenberg basically agrees with his Frankfurt forebears that politics in the traditional sense is well under the control of the system. The extent of conscious

activity in connection with technology, challenging designs and modifying practices of use, is real politics because it touches directly on the
operation of structures of power in modern societies and presents an
immanent challenge to the hold of that system. When Feenberg makes
the case for technical politics, one of the things he is saying is that this is
the only, or certainly the main, viable form of real politics today.

There is, then, a continuous thread that connects Feenberg's involvement with the student protests in the 1960s to his identification of technology as the principal locus of contemporary politics. Digital technology
has opened up what seemed to be closed off, namely, the possibility of a
political challenge to the system that, just a few decades ago, had been
called 'technocracy'. It is perhaps ironic that that this opening appears
in the very dimension of social life that had seemed to be most strongly
associated with the dominance of the system.

Moreover, the changes to technology associated with the move to
digital culture involve alterations not only to the productive or economic dimension of society. The rise of computers and of other digital
techniques has changed the way that technology relates to culture and
meaning. In effect, it raises the question of whether there is a single continuous meaning to the idea of technology, a definition that transcends
such discrepancies and links all of its various instances. Is there something inherently or essentially technical that connects the Manchester–
Liverpool railway of 1830 to 2019's iPhone XS? According to Feenberg,
the answer is not straightforward. There is an essential thread running
through all instances of technology, but it is only ever encountered in a
distinctive, contemporary social construction.

When he writes that technology has a historical essence, Feenberg
takes the important step of incorporating a sociological element into
the philosophical definition of technology. It is this move that enables
him to comprehend the changes just discussed as *part of the meaning*
of technology, and on this basis to identify the possibility of technical
politics, while at the same time retaining a perspective grounded in
critical theory. The latter, as we have seen, involves suspicion of instrumental reason and often identifies this with the essence of technology.
The fact that Feenberg continues to invoke ideas formulated in the pre-
digital context sometimes creates the impression of a prevarication on
this point, something that is discussed at greater length in what follows.
A key contention of this book, however, is that this is a misreading of his
work, which is in fact avowedly and consistently anti-essentialist, in the
sense that it refuses to identify technology with instrumentalism. The
critique Feenberg makes of technology is premised not on the notion
that it is instrumental in essence, but on the empirical observation that
when it serves the ends of social domination this tends to coincide with
a pronounced instrumentalism in its design. This explains why earlier,

essentialist philosophies sometimes 'ring true' even though their fundamental premises are false.

This is not to deny that there are problems at this point in his theory, however. I will suggest that rather than prevarication there is a hesitation in Feenberg's approach, by which I mean that once he has identified technology's role in social domination with its instrumental aspects, he does not recognise that it can also be biased in other ways. The relationship between technology in which the instrumental dimension is more pronounced and the social employment of technology to exploit and dominate both people and nature may well be much as he describes, as a matter of contemporary social historical fact. But it is important to notice that, consistent with the anti-essentialist approach, this leaves open the twin possibilities of progressive yet nakedly instrumental technique and the use of aestheticised and ostensibly meaningful designs in strategies of exploitation and manipulation.

This raises the question of how regressive and positive features are to be discerned when discussing technologies in context. Since technology is political, indeed is co-extensive with the political in the sense described above, this is a vital question for the critical theory of technology. One hazard attendant on any theory that views technology as the singular locus of conscious struggles over social power is that of taking an aesthetic index as the obvious route to target problematic designs. Machines that clearly prioritise function over form, the efficient realisation of a purpose over qualitative questions concerning the character of use, will then seem to be obviously contentious, while those that get inserted more or less seamlessly into social situations and perhaps even serve overt communicative ends will tend to disappear from view. The ease with which technical politics might fall into this is one of the reasons why the critical theory of technology warrants examination and critique. It is perhaps especially important to clarify the aesthetic dimension of the theory, to make it into a primary means for addressing technologies as socially problematic, even before they become politically contentious.

The main point of critique pursued in this book concerns the Adornian principle of non-identity as the basic point of departure for critical theory. My suggestion is that Feenberg succeeds, in the theory of technical politics, in placing technology firmly within the problematics of identity and representation. It is when technology design stitches a new device, technique or machine into the web of currently accepted identifications and social meanings that it serves power most effectively. This may not coincide with it behaving instrumentally or with the proliferation of the kinds of 'symptom' associated with industrial-era technologies, like physical harm to workers or egregious resource depletion. Contemporary technical politics concerns the kind of 'doubling' that occurs when an app, for example, contributes to an ongoing process of subjectification, condemning people to a narrowly specified course of action rather than promoting or accommodating reflection that might open up alternative personal trajectories. Such nodal points in the operation of specific technologies can be related to impositions of identity and conformity onto social subjects, and technical politics ought to focus on creating opportunities for alternative subjectivations, by urging design changes that reduce dependency and enhance informed technology use.

This question of how to diagnose entanglements of specific designs with webs of social power also has a bearing on the kind of technical-political action that ought to be considered 'progressive'. Feenberg tends to identify positive developments in technical politics with action that points towards reconciliation of subject and object in a changed civilisation, in which technology has been redesigned to serve the interests of culture and communication rather than the narrow, instrumental goal of enhanced productive efficiency. Feenberg's preference here is informed by his affinity with Marcuse, for whom society is an organic whole that has been split apart by capitalism and awaits re-unification. For Adorno, in contrast, any politics based directly on the search for reconciliation of subject and object risks imposing its own identitarian demands on both of them.

Feenberg takes from Marcuse the principle that critique should move beyond the retrospective exercise of judgement to explain what has happened in the past as a negative consequence of the totally administered life, in order to actively promote reflection aimed at illuminating a course to something better in the future. He alleges that Adorno and other critical theorists evade crucial questions when they fail to take this step, effectively regressing behind some kind of mealy-mouthed Kantian moralism – condemning everything while refusing to say what should be done instead. I argue that in his rush to identify and affirm positive, present potential, Feenberg makes a pre-emptive move towards politics that cannot but leave unanswered questions in its wake.

The critical purpose of this book, therefore, is to address some of those questions with the Adornian principle of non-identity in mind, not with the aim of knocking Feenberg's theory down but rather in an attempt to support his efforts to identify and draw out the political significance in much of what is going on in contemporary digital culture. The result is that, while we reach slightly different conclusions, I argue nonetheless that Feenberg's critical perspective serves as a much more productive approach than the available alternatives in contemporary thought about technology.

3 Technical politics

My account of Feenberg begins by identifying his central question with that of Marx. Their common problematic concerns the contradictions of the capitalist social formation and how they result in the transition to a society that takes the maximum degree of individual human self-realisation as its organising principle. Chapter 1 introduces the idea of technical politics as, first and foremost, an attempt on Feenberg's part to solve a fundamental dilemma of Marxism which, despite its urgent and as yet unresolved character and the enormous quantity of Marx scholarship over the past two centuries, is rarely addressed head-on anywhere. Feenberg not only engages with it but, in the theory of technical politics, presents an ambitious solution.

In his theory of history, Marx (1970) locates technology in the material infrastructure of society, among its productive forces, which he considers more fundamental to the explanation of social change than superstructural features like ideas or legal rights. Living in society, 'men inevitably enter into definite relations, which are independent of their will, namely relations of production appropriate to a given stage in the development of their material forces of production' (1970: 20). The latter include technology and tend to expand in productive power over the course of the historical process. This development of the productive forces is a condition of possibility of the transition to a socialist society, because that society has to be able to produce great quantities of material wealth if it is to facilitate the multitude of projects entailed by its emphasis on individuals' self-development. Marxism therefore identifies technology development as the key to historical progress. Moreover, within this overarching historical process, capitalism is the social formation that most accelerates technology development. Overturning the constraints of tradition, the dynamism of the capitalist economy means that it is always innovating and producing new, more productive machines. The place of capitalism in Marx's historical eschatology, immediately prior to socialism, is no accident: capitalism creates the material conditions, including the technical foundations, that make socialism possible.

However, Marx also describes in detail how technology in capitalist society is shaped to serve the interests of the capitalist class in their struggle against the mass of the people, who have to operate the machines. He shows that the principal motivation for capitalists to introduce new techniques is not to improve efficiency, or even to enhance their competitiveness, but rather to act against their employees. From the perspective of the individual capitalist, machinery is primarily an opportunity to reduce reliance on workers and to thwart their efforts to take control of the production process. For this reason, capitalist machinery is designed to oppress workers and to contribute to their domination rather than their self-realisation.

The dilemma here is that capitalist technology is held to be both shaped to be unpleasant for workers *and* the foundation for a socialist society, in which arduous toil is replaced by freely associated productive activity.

Feenberg discusses how the Soviets failed to address this problem and instead pursued a strategy of copying capitalist technology, combined for many years with a militaristic social organisation of the workplace. In consequence, the experience of living and working in Soviet society was no less unpleasant than life in a capitalist one, with the changed relations of ownership and control over production becoming something of an abstraction from the standpoint of the ordinary worker. Marx's paradox, then, had a toxic practical legacy in the twentieth century.

Feenberg draws the lesson that technology is one of the things that has to change as a part of the transition to a superior, socialist society. What he calls 'civilizational change' involves not only a break with the capitalist economy but an equally, if not more, profound shift at the level of material culture, and technology is implicated on both levels. The working class, as conceived by Marx, are not the privileged agents of this work of transformation. Instead, the struggle to change technology is more diffuse and concerns everyone who is subject to the operations of power in modern society. Drawing on critical theory's synthesis of Marx and Weber, Feenberg argues that the authority of technology discussed by Marx and Engels is not limited to the industrial workplace but spreads throughout society and culture.

Technology, in this argument, is not only shaped by capitalist interests and antithetical to workers' well-being but is also a key agent of societal rationalisation. While the development of technology remains, as Marx maintained, ultimately progressive, it is also shaped by the tendency towards intensified use of instrumental reason to enhance efficiency and, as Weber (1974) had shown, a correspondingly diminished role for meaning in social processes. In this analysis, technology is reified so that it appears to be the 'best solution' in any given workplace scenario, and resisting it becomes near-synonymous with irrationality.

By following his critical theory forebears and making this synthesis of Marx with Weber, Feenberg only seems to have doubled his difficulty. Somehow, technology must be the vehicle to a better society, yet it is also shaped by the capitalist interest in domination *and* societal rationalisation. Feenberg's solution is the theory of ambivalence: technology is both biased in the ways just described and remains the locus of a set of capabilities that could set humanity free. Technical politics mediates the poles of this contradiction, with the actions of social agents competing over the meaning of technology in a struggle that is now invested with political significance.

Recognising the activity of a range of social groups whose actions subvert or even democratise technology design and use as political, Feenberg opens up a theoretical space that both bears upon the very meaning of technology and helps to address Marx's problem. The transition to socialism now includes a technical dimension in the sense that, just as socialist culture and institutions need to be prefigured as part of counter-hegemonic struggle, so its technological foundations can also be presaged by struggles waged in the present. Where hackers produce software to support striking workers by automating denial-of-service attacks on company servers, or when patients' groups demand that drug testing regimes be liberalised to allow them access to experimental treatments, Feenberg identifies the seeds of a socialist technology. Where these struggles are successful they bend technology design and technical practices to human ends, and the result is 'democratic' or 'subversive rationalisation'.

Technical politics consists of interventions that affect technology in ways that counter its existing bias. Chapter 2 discusses Feenberg's account of the bias of technology under capitalism, which he calls 'formal' bias and rigorously distinguishes from the substantive version propounded by essentialist scholars. Feenberg's inclusion of social factors in the philosophical definition of technology is in evidence here. According to his argument, technology is formally biased only when it is placed in a determinate social context. Cases of substantive bias, when a design is inherently detrimental to the interests of a specific social group (or even straightforwardly inhuman), are outliers. Yet technology never really exists as such outside of social contexts, and so a definition of it that disregarded that context would itself be a mere abstraction. Feenberg rejects essentialist theories, like those of Jacques Ellul (1964) and Martin Heidegger (2013), on that basis.

At the same time, though, essentialist critics identify bias in technology with certain traits with which it has long been strongly associated – in particular, the instrumental reduction of sometimes complex and meaningful situations to 'problems' with a single solution. Efficiency is often associated with this kind of narrowing of focus onto the attainment of a clearly defined goal by the most expeditious means, and its pursuit is open to criticism when it leads to the neglect of important neighbouring features of the world. This leads Feenberg to acknowledge that substantive critique sometimes has purchase, but, for him, this is a consequence of technology's historically contingent role in modern rationalisation and its shaping by factors specific to that context, rather than of its substantive character as technology.

The chapter concludes by arguing that Feenberg fails to follow through on this argument, with the result that he rejects the substantivist baby with the essentialist bathwater. In fact, technology is always substantively biased, and this insight is made possible by Feenberg's own move of including a social element in the definition. The substantive properties of technology that make it biased are not always the ones operative in capitalist modernity, which means that the question of its bias needs to be uncoupled from its purported instrumentalising qualities.

In short, removing one kind of capitalist bias by making technology more meaningful or pleasurable to use may well lead to another kind; it will never make technology neutral. Feenberg knows this, of course, but does not, it seems to me, take full advantage of his own insight when reflecting on socialist technology, which will have to have its own kind of substantive bias.

The third chapter turns to Feenberg's concept of technical politics, which, as I have suggested above, is perhaps his central theoretical innovation. The idea of technical politics involves a further theoretical synthesis, this time of social constructivism with Ernesto Laclau and Chantal Mouffe's (1985) theory of hegemony and radical democracy. In a number of influential works published in the 1980s, scholars in the new discipline of science and technology studies (STS) established the notion that social groups shape technologies by competing to attach their own preferred meanings to them in the early phases of their development (e.g. Bijker and Hughes 1989). These labelling processes involve rival constituencies identifying capacities in new technologies that might be used to solve problems in a way that is relevant to their needs or interests. Perhaps the most important insight here, from Feenberg's perspective, is that this process is competitive, because this is a clue to its political character.

If constructivists generally overlooked wider questions, like the social consequences of a particular group's success in gaining control of a technology, Feenberg insists that disputes over what a technology is for commonly have far-reaching consequences that should not be bracketed out. More importantly still, the fact that such disputes can occur at all, and even seem to be happening more often, suggests that the totally administered, rationalised society described by Adorno and Horkheimer (1997) and Marcuse (1964) may have come unstuck. Dissent is surfacing close to the heart of that social formation, in connection with its most reified, authoritative element. This development is seized upon by Feenberg as the fulfilment of Marcuse's idea that technocracy might be transformed from within by the development of an alternative technology.

Another fertile aspect of STS exploited by Feenberg is its emphasis on language and descriptive operations that represent technologies in such a way as to affect how they are initially perceived, which has consequences for how they turn out and are presented to the wider public. Technology design then emerges as a contest played out in games of description and counter-description, which are described in detail by STS scholars, albeit in a way that nearly always neglects the issue of social power. Drawing on Laclau and Mouffe's (1985) highly discursive conception of politics, Feenberg reinterprets these processes as agonistic articulations occurring within the parameters set by capitalist hegemony. Technology, in this terminology, is 'coded' in its design process, and competing social groups seek to make their own articulations of this code dominant, or hegemonic.

Technical politics, then, is played out through multiple local struggles to articulate technology in a dual sense: (1) to provide the dominant expression or representation of a technology, so that it comes to be associated with some purposes rather than others; and (2) in so doing, to connect a given design to the global meaning of technology itself, in a move that alters the prevailing conception of what technology is and, importantly, what it might be in the future. The latter is the hegemonic codification of technology, which Feenberg takes to be crystallised in the works of essentialist philosophers, even if they are wrong to believe that this is all that technology can be.

The idea of technical politics is the centrepiece of Feenberg's theory, providing his entire intervention with its rationale. The theoretical synthesis of STS and politicised post-structuralism is ingenious, and it restores politics and the necessity of radical social change, in particular radical democratic transformation, to the centre of critical theory's concerns. Chapter 3 describes why Feenberg identifies such political promise in contemporary popular interventions in a variety of technical fields of activity. However, the chapter also lodges a number of reservations.

First, the aggregation of multiple local struggles over technology need not ever amount to the kind of sweeping, wholesale system change implicit in Feenberg's reference to 'civilizational change'. Second, the theory seems to exaggerate the extent to which technical politics simply is politics, in which case technology and contests over the meaning of technology are the only available way for people to challenge the social system. This last impression is re-enforced by Feenberg's characterisation of the current technical hegemony in terms that are drawn from essentialist scholarship: if that is an accurate account then the technocratic system as a whole is largely intact and its technology is, paradoxically, the only chink in its armour. Third, Feenberg's move to view these social interventions as a progressive form of politics may be peremptory in the sense that it leaves out of account all those actors and social groups who, for various reasons, are not actively involved in changing technology but are excluded from its development and use. Why such exclusion happens is a sociological rather than a political question, and it could be argued that it is one that should be integral to any critical theory of technology.

Chapter 4 turns to the notion that technical politics has an important aesthetic dimension. As seen above, Feenberg takes from Marx (1983) the idea of an intrinsic connection between social power and the sensory configuration of the human creature. This relationship is, to a large extent, mediated through technology and technology design, since changes here tend to be determinate for historical variation in the texture and feel of lived or sensed experience. Feenberg's analysis of aestheticisation starts from the observation that, historically, all technology has been attentive to the question of how it fits with the rest of human activity. This concerns questions of meaning – specifically, how individual technical objects symbolise their function to putative operators. Such public symbolisation processes serve to situate objects in wider webs of significance and meaning. The way that technology design addresses this issue in any given society will have a bearing on how technics and technique cohere with the wider cultural context and on what is meant by technology as a whole.

All technology has this symbolic dimension, but how it interacts with technical functionality is historically variable. According to Feenberg, what distinguishes the technology of capitalist modernity is that, unlike other cultures, it neglects this aspect of technology design, presenting its users with a peculiarly austere kind of technology. It is in this context that technology in modern societies is perceived (and theorised) as a narrowly instrumental, even brutal, dimension of society and often regarded as something that needs to be contained and limited to specific areas of activity. Feenberg emphasises that this is a contingent meaning, however, and points to other cultures in which technology represents other, positive values.

In traditional societies, for example, it was common for people to decorate tools and machines, a practice that demonstrated their incorporation into the weave of cultural life. Similarly, facility with a particular kind of tool would often be associated with a social role or identity, with the consequence that the user and the tool would be held in a certain kind of esteem by the rest of the community. Residual traces of this more organic relationship between individuals, technology and culture can be discerned in modern, even industrial settings, where workers continue to decorate factory tools and some technical professions maintain a collective sense of themselves as vocations. These things are harder to sustain under modern conditions because technology is designed in a way that is neglectful of its symbolic aspect, reflecting (and contributing to) the fact that it has become abstracted from society and often seems to sit outside of culture.

Feenberg comprehends this difference in terms of his theory of 'instrumentalisation', which is the focus of Chapter 5. Instrumentalisation has primary and secondary moments. Primary instrumentalisation refers to the historically continuous sub-stratum of human interaction with the physical and natural environment, which always involves a certain kind of violence associated with the displacement of items from their natural locations and their reduction to those aspects that are used to achieve a human purpose. There is a strong resonance between primary instrumentalisation and essentialist theories of technology, but Feenberg emphasises that no technology consists purely of its primary instrumentalisations. Technology always also includes a second moment, in which it is articulated to meaning-making activities that constitute the society and culture of which it is a part. This is where Feenberg incorporates historical and social factors into the definition of technology. Just as when he includes instrumentality and communication and the opposition between them as factors internal to technology development, so here he performs a kind of introjection whereby essentialist and constructivist elements are made to co-mingle in a single conception of what technology is.

The elements in this definition, then, are in play whenever there are disputes over the meaning of any given technical artefact. Feenberg maintains that capitalist modernity is characterised by a uniquely stark, stripped-down version of secondary instrumentalisation, so that its technology is marked by a tendency to erode and undermine the compensatory aspect of secondary instrumentalisation, revealing what appears to some as the violent heart of technical endeavour. However, technical politics makes it clear that capitalist technology runs up against an internal limit, in the sense that no merely instrumental technology is actually possible, and other forces, internal to technology development itself, will necessarily counter this tendency and attempt to insert symbolic mediations that mollify primary instrumentalisation.

The notion that technology includes, as part of its internal rational structure, a meaningful aspect that might be expanded upon and developed is central to Feenberg's suggestion that, contrary to Adornian pessimism, it might be possible to construct utopia from here, the nerve centre of technocracy. Moreover, by identifying democratic technical politics as the means through which secondary instrumentalisation might be expanded and infused with alternative meanings beyond the narrow pursuit of ends, he presents a vision of such change as democratic, rather than carried through by a progressive technical elite, as in Marcuse's version.

Feenberg is particularly critical of Adorno for failing to include such a positive moment in his version of critical theory, calling the latter's refusal to countenance utopia an 'evasion' that renders his theory largely irrelevant. In the final chapter I suggest that the real problem here is one that Feenberg himself does not fully escape – namely, that there is an epistemological problem for critique as a way of identifying social problems, which can be brought into relief by using utopia as a method for thinking the future. The book concludes with the suggestion that, especially in his own refusal to theorise the substantively biasing aspects of progressive technology, Feenberg's technical politics also does not deliver on its utopian promise. Notwithstanding this, his theory offers crucial resources with which to move in that direction, and for that reason alone it demands our attention.

Notes

1 This view is confirmed by Feenberg's pre-eminent position in most anthologies and in discussions at all the relevant symposia on philosophy of technology, as well as the pride of place assigned to his pieces in prestigious collections like the one edited by Robert Scharff and Val Dusek (2003). He has secured a prominent place for Marxian thought within one of the most important sub-fields of contemporary philosophy, an accomplishment all the more remarkable at a time when left-leaning academics have been largely excluded from many disciplines, including philosophy and sociology. While two edited collections (Veak 2006; Arnold and Michel 2017) have been devoted to his work, I believe this is the first monograph study.
2 This photograph can be accessed at: www.sfu.ca/~andrewf/books/may68.pdf. Accessed 9 December 2019.
3 'Adorno was unsympathetic to any form of revolutionary action, interpreting it as blind to its own motives and naïve about its likely consequences' (O'Connor 2012: 13).
4 Lorenz Jäger reports that Horkheimer 'stuck demonstratively to the side of the United States, whose mission to save the world from the dangers of Eastern Communism he had made entirely his own' (2004: 197–198).
5 Adorno was Habermas's doctoral supervisor, as Marcuse was Feenberg's.

1

Critical theory and technology

Feenberg's critical theory of technology is to a large extent constructed through a synthesis of concepts from several predecessor theories, each of them important to his work in different ways, and each a source of concepts that he modifies in order to incorporate them into his own syncretic framework. This chapter describes the overarching rationale of Feenberg's intellectual project, with reference to some of these sources. It suggests that the result is a new system in which concepts take on altered significance and are made to do quite different work than they did in the earlier theories. Exploring in detail the new philosophy that emerges is the principal task of this book.

Looking at the way he engages with the ideas of Marx, Weber and earlier critical theorists makes it possible to identify the problems Feenberg is trying to solve with reference to what he sees as the crucial lacunae, errors and unsolved problems in his predecessors' work. It also clarifies the meanings of key terms in Feenberg's own corpus, for example when Feenberg introduces the idea of 'democratic rationalisation', a phrase that might seem almost oxymoronic if its terms were not properly contextualised in the works of scholars who assigned them specific meanings. Moreover, to establish the key criteria against which Feenberg's work as a whole ought to be judged it is important to grasp his main theoretical and practical priorities, and these emerge most clearly when he engages with other work in the critical theory tradition. Even his choice of key sources is itself revealing of Feenberg's overall problematic and of the conceptual innovations he introduces.

Feenberg's project is deeply informed by Marx and Marxism, though his main questions, which concern the politics of technology design, were completely overlooked in Marx's own work. Of special importance is Marx's concept of human self-realisation, a theme that informs all of Marx's work from his earliest writings, through *Capital* to his final reflections on the historical process (Stedman-Jones 2016). Marx was concerned with the social and historical conditions in which every human individual might be enabled to flourish and fulfil their potential. He referred to this as the 'all round development of each individual' (Marx and Engels 1982: 117). He speculated (infrequently, it should be noted) that in a society with advanced technology and socialist economic relations people would be freed from drudgery and enforced labour so that everyone could cultivate all their talents, writing plays in the morning, hunting in the afternoon and doing a bit of literary criticism after dinner.

This vision, which is a normative shibboleth of socialist ideology, is essentially preserved in Feenberg's critical theory, where it is technology as much as capitalist economic and social forms of organisation that prevents it from being realised. The paradox that technology, which Marx believed made his vision feasible by greatly enhancing human productive power, should be one of the forces ranged against the self-realisation of the species is already there in Marx's writings. Feenberg's innovation is to tackle it head-on, and his whole theory can be read as an attempt to resolve this problem in Marx's work.

Marx's problematic was taken over in the twentieth century by the Frankfurt School of critical theory, and this movement is the second key source for Feenberg's theory. Famously, thinkers of the Frankfurt School combined Marx's insights on capitalism and the new forms of authority and social power associated with it, including the authority of machinery, with Max Weber's thesis that capitalist modernity is a social formation in the grip of 'rationalisation'. The increased emphasis on instrumental efficiency that runs through modern institutional forms combines with a capitalist economy to produce new intensities of domination and associated human anguish. This leads Adorno and Horkheimer to characterise modern capitalism as a 'total society which embraces all relations and emotions' and eliminates any vestige of individuality by imposing 'isolation in the forcibly united collectivity' (1997: 36).[1]

Technology clearly plays an important role in any such negative characterisation of modern society, and Feenberg considers the Frankfurt School thesis 'dystopian'. Like Heidegger (another important source for Feenberg), Adorno and Horkheimer find technology implicated in the worst excesses of a social system based on quantification as the basis of strategies of control whose operations are inimical to meaning, even though the latter is clearly an essential dimension of human existence. However, Feenberg's main influence here is Herbert Marcuse, who was famously associated with the Frankfurt School and shared many of Adorno and Horkheimer's views on history, society and culture, but consistently differed from them politically.

In the years after World War Two in particular, Marcuse argued that the negative image of modernity advanced by other Frankfurt School theorists was excessively pessimistic and in some ways a regression behind Marx, who had always emphasised capitalism's vulnerability to explosive social contradictions, as well as its facility for producing fresh strategies to maintain itself. Marcuse's optimism about the potential of the student movement, noted in the Introduction, contrasted markedly with Horkheimer's more pessimistic view, as did his more measured view of the Eastern bloc. In his *One-Dimensional Man* (1964) Marcuse presented an image of modern societies that was similar to the world of total administration depicted in Adorno and Horkheimer's work, but he also identified positive political potential in a new generation of young technologists, who he thought might be inclined to design technics for a better civilisation (1964: 227–229). This idea is an important launching-off point for Feenberg's theory.

To develop this notion further, Feenberg engages with a third branch of scholarship, namely the constructivism associated with science and technology studies (STS), which came to prominence in the academy in the 1980s. Work in this school focused on the underdetermined character of technological artefacts, especially in their development phase (e.g. Bijker *et al* 1989). No strictly technical imperative leads from the discovery of wheels, pedals, handlebars, even pneumatic tyres, to what we know as the bicycle. Rather, the presence of such physical elements has to be parsed through the opinions and verbal behaviours of 'relevant social agents' for such an object to be produced. The meanings that shape technologies are social products, while the uses to which they are put emerge retrospectively: technologies and the problems they solve emerge in the course of the same social processes.

In constructivism Feenberg finds the opening he needs for critical theory to build on Marcuse's insight. If technology is not historically determinate but rather itself a dependent variable of the social process then it must be possible for human beings to influence its design. Constructivist studies of technology describe the social shaping of technology, showing how the beliefs and values of social groups affect the design of nascent technologies, especially in their development phase. Critical theorists had argued that technology framed modern society and culture, limiting the range of meaningful human experience. Marcuse's suggestion is that technical transformation might be the way to address these issues. Constructivism equips Feenberg with tools for the development of a political theory of technology applicable to the question of radical socialist transformation and thereby enables him to address the unresolved paradox in Marx's thought on the issue. Each of these sources, and the terms of Feenberg's engagement with them, is addressed in this chapter.

1 Feenberg's Marx

Feenberg shares Marx's core conviction that, 'the goal of a good society should be to enable human beings to realize their potentialities to the fullest' (2002: 19). According to Marx, this society was coming within reach of humanity, largely as a result of the astonishing rate of development of productive power made possible in the nineteenth century by industrial technology. Industrial society was so wealthy that for the first time in history, universal human self-realisation was becoming a practical possibility.

Marx was one of the first philosophers to place technology at the centre of his understanding of the human condition. Many of his arguments, while controversial when he made them, have become almost common sense today. In particular, Marx was the first to suggest that the historical process rests centrally on the development of the productive forces. He famously argued that human experience, culture and civilisation turn not, as his contemporaries tended to argue, on providence or the unfolding of some spiritual purpose, but on the material practices that people engage in to produce and reproduce their material conditions of existence. Technology, or the means humans use to manipulate the world in order to extract what they need from it to survive and thrive, is central to this, and changes to technical capacity, in particular those that improve productivity, drive social change.

At the same time, Marx was also a critic of technology, especially nineteenth-century industrial machinery. He argued that in the capitalist organisation of production,

> all means for the development of production undergo a dialectical inversion so that they become means of domination and exploitation of the producers. (1990: 799)

According to his theory of history, capitalism is a necessary phase of development that human societies must pass through if they are to reach the level of productivity required to sustain socialism. As this citation indicates, however, it is not a pleasant experience for most people because in this society only a small number of people enjoy the benefits of the new levels of productive power. For the majority, the new machines are a source of suffering, both physical and in terms of changes to social existence that correspond to the domination and exploitation Marx refers to here. Ultimately, though, Marx writes in the *Grundrisse* that the technology designed to dominate workers reduces necessary labour to a minimum and, for this reason, 'will redound to the benefit of emancipated labour and is the condition of its emancipation' (1981: 701).

In *Capital*, Marx describes the capitalist development of industrial technology as passing through two phases. The first ran roughly from the mid-seventeenth to the late eighteenth century and was based on the workshop. Workers who had formerly worked in their own homes using craft techniques and personalised implements found themselves reduced to the level of operating machines owned by capitalists. They lost their craft relation with the labour process, which they no longer controlled, and became deskilled. They also lost connection with the finished product, only engaging with the part of it that directly involved their efforts. Marx writes that this phase: 'converts the worker into a crippled monstrosity ... the individual himself is divided up, and transformed into the automatic motor of a detailed operation' (1990: 481).

With the spread of steam power in the early nineteenth century, however, a further change to the organisation of the factory occurs. Human workers cease to be the power source, and the various machines are hooked up into a single system, in which the worker's role is further diminished to providing 'supplementary assistance'. From this point on, machines constitute an 'automatic system' which grows 'spontaneously on a material basis ... adequate for it' (1990: 504). Workers become just a part of the industrial machine system; their activity is planned and imposed from outside by the mechanism. All parts of the process are subject to the same 'technical law' (1990: 465).

This development involves the emergence of a new form of authority, invested in the machinery itself. Marx's lifelong collaborator Friedrich Engels clarified the role of machinery in social domination in the following terms:

> The automatic machinery of a big factory is much more despotic than the small capitalists who employ workers have ever been ... If man, by dint of his knowledge and inventive genius, has subdued the forces of nature, the latter avenge themselves on him, in so far as he employs them, to a veritable despotism independent of all social organisation. (Marx and Engels 1958: 637)

Technology here embodies social functions that are wider in their significance than merely enhancing productivity and efficiency. The machines are authoritative in the sense that they represent, to their human users and to society as whole, the only viable course of action. Their rise to power, so to speak, is a function of the fact that in order to maximise its productive capabilities the workplace must be tyrannised by the articulated, steam-powered system. The human consequences of these developments include further deskilling and reduction of workers' control over the production process, and their subordination to a new source of authority. These developments appear to the people involved as the inevitable consequence of new technology, as the price to be paid for its almost unimaginable expansion of productive power.

When reflecting on its historical significance, Marx enthused about this development of the productive forces, arguing that for the first time in human history the species might reach a stage at which each individual could fulfil their potential. If the productive power of the industrial system could be freed from the constraints of having to produce for profit and instead be directed to producing to meet real human needs, he argued, then everyone would be free to devote their time to leisure and self-cultivation. The transition was deeply problematic, however, because of the multiple entanglements of technology and its liberating potential with existing society and culture.

Feenberg's critical theory of technology and his notion of technical politics are situated within this, Marx's problematic. Focusing particularly on what Marx has to say about technology, we are confronted with the problem, alluded to above, that Marx is both an enthusiast for technology, viewing it as carrying humanity forward to a superior form of social life, *and* deeply concerned about it as a force that diminishes the meaning of human activity while becoming a locus of domination exerting control over human actions.[2]

Focusing on Marx's critical comments on technology, Feenberg identifies three lines of argument, which he calls the design, process and product critiques (2002: 46–48). The design critique concerns the way that technology is constructed and shaped to serve particular social purposes. Feenberg cites Marx when he points out that 'it would be possible to write a whole history of the inventions made since 1830 for the sole purpose of supplying capital with weapons against working class revolt' (1990: 593). According to Marx, capitalists are motivated to produce technology that is harmful to workers in ways that underscore two further lines of critique. Machines are weapons against workers' combining to oppose and resist capitalists at the point of production, since they foster job insecurity. They are also introduced to reduce the cost of production, and this is commonly about reducing the wage bill by shedding employees and getting machinery to do the work instead. The resulting diminution of quality in the work process itself, as workers become mere 'assistants', is what Feenberg calls Marx's 'process critique'.[3]

The third, product critique is present wherever Marx criticises wasteful or foolish employments of technical means. This particularly concerns the production of commodities that correspond to artificial needs or even to things that are actually detrimental to human interests. An obvious target for the product critique might be the manufacture of weapons systems that are too powerful ever to be used, since this seems to be a misdirection of human technical capabilities.[4] The category of artificial needs raises the question of what 'real' needs are and how they are to be defined. For now it is important to notice that the design critique of technology occupies a privileged position in relation to the other two. This is because it is only *as designed* that technology is harmful to humans, wasteful or otherwise damaging.

If Marx assigns explanatory priority to machines and implements it is not because they are completely exempt from being themselves socially shaped. There are numerous references in Marx's writings to social factors causing technology change to happen, even selecting specific technical designs. Describing the social changes that affected the cotton industry in eighteenth-century England, for instance, Marx writes that 'the revolution in cotton-spinning called forth the invention of the gin' (1990: 505). As Alan Wood (2004) points out, the fact that technology turns out to explain social change even when it comes after it in time is not as implausible as it sounds.[5] It does raise the question, though, of its entanglement with other, supposedly more malleable social factors.

Notwithstanding this, and the comment Feenberg cites from *Capital* above, there is not much evidence in Marx's texts that he devoted any great critical energy to the social processes that shaped technology. Marx does not seem to see any paradox in his advocacy of technology as progress on one side and his critique of technology as regressive under capitalism on the other. His references to 'dialectical inversion' and 'redounding' in the sections cited above are masks on a potentially thorny question that he did not address directly.[6] Feenberg's project of developing a politics of technology design, or technical politics, is an attempt to make sense of this issue.

2 Sources of critique

If technology design is a dimension of the transition to a superior form of social life then Feenberg's challenge in his critical theory of technology is to deepen the critical perspective on technology while maintaining a belief in science and in technology as basically progressive. He needs to clarify what is wrong with capitalist technology in a way that is sufficiently profound and comports in particular with the critical explanation of modernity, while at the same time leaving a way open to changing it and preserving the basic Marxist belief in technology's potential to be a force for human emancipation. To achieve this, he clarifies what is wrong with modern technology by drawing on insights from earlier thinkers both within and outside the Marxist tradition. Of particular importance here are the Frankfurt School critical theorists, who examined the implications of Marx's core historical and economic propositions for twentieth-century culture. Simply put, Feenberg tries to use their ideas without lapsing into their stark condemnation of modern technology.

Critical theory elaborates on three aspects of Marx that are of particular importance to Feenberg's project. First, it builds on Marx and Engels' argument, discussed above, about the relationship between technology and authority, showing that in capitalist modernity the two are linked through a mediating concept of social rationality. In the works of Adorno, Horkheimer and Marcuse, instrumental reason is the force that shapes the modern experience of the world. The Frankfurt School authors present a critique of modern science as the application of this kind of reasoning to the understanding of nature and the physical universe. They complain that this conceals or obscures aspects of the world and of experience that elude its in-built orientation towards measurement and regularity.

This line of argument builds on Marx's discussion of the sensory configuration of the human creature and its modification over the course of the historical process. In early writings Marx described the 'sheer estrangement' in bourgeois society of all human senses in 'the sense of *having*' (1981: 94).[7] In the rationalised version of capitalism, humans are geared up, so to speak, to relate narrowly to objects in the world in terms of what they can be used for or how they may be consumed, with a corresponding neglect of the full range of their potentialities. Underlying this perspective is the idea of a distortion of human and technical potentials as a result of what Feenberg calls 'formal rationality'.[8] The source for this idea is not Marx but Georg Lukàcs.

Lukàcs's version of Marxism, as formulated in his 1923 (1981) classic *History and Class Consciousness*, describes Marx's philosophy as 'the theory of totality'. On his reading of Marx, the standpoint of the proletariat is unique because, while throughout history people who work have created social reality, industrial workers are the first group of such people who might become fully aware of their role and its implications. Whereas previous labouring classes have been in various ways fragmented and held apart by different social structures, in industrial capitalism their ontological role as creators is matched by their potential epistemic one as socially omniscient. Because workers are thrown together in a largely homogeneous social mass, sharing key experiences and a common culture, the working class are in a position to comprehend both the world they have created and their role in creating it. Thus, their self-emancipation is almost inevitable once they have access to the truth: why should they continue to produce enormous wealth, only for it to be appropriated by the bosses?

The main obstacle to proletarian self-emancipation, elaborated in Lukàcs's account, is reification. This idea builds on Marx's account of fetishism in *Capital*, according to which the extraction of value in commodity production results in a strange inversion whereby objects that are produced for sale on the market become charged with a special liveliness, while the people whose labour produced them are exhausted and spent, coming to seem in their own eyes lifeless and inert. In reification the agents of history perceive themselves as incapable of effecting real change yet perceive their own collective products as vitally fascinating. Lukàcs generalises this analysis onto the whole of modern culture, arguing that reification is the central problem of modernity, resulting in the pervasive belief that the world is made up of causally interrelated objects whose logic overrides subjective considerations of quality, meaning and value.[9]

Lukàcs's work was the focus of Feenberg's first monograph study (his 1981) and these ideas are central to the critical theory of technology. In that work Feenberg suggests that the most questionable element in Lukàcs's theory is also his 'most original and fruitful' point, namely 'the discovery that linking all the phenomena of capitalist society Marx criticises, from fetishism to mechanisation and crises, there is a common structure, a pattern constituted by the imposition of formal rationality on the social world' (1981: 76). Reification is a distorted perception of the world, then, that runs through modern science and culture and fosters a disposition to identify an instrumental pattern and connection between facts as the hallmark of a realistic understanding of the natural world and human social processes alike.[10]

Lukàcs's idea of a distinctively instrumental reason as shaping modern experience is taken up by and becomes one of the unifying themes of Frankfurt School critical theory, uniting Adorno and Marcuse.[11] Instrumental or means-end reasoning is said to underpin modern science and to be implemented in the technology associated with it. Centrally, then, science purports to show the world as structured according to laws of causation that describe behavioural regularities. Science as such is true, in the sense that it consists, as Karl Popper (1989) would have it, in the open-ended refinement of propositions that are formulated to ensure they are falsifiable in principle. However, for Frankfurt School theorists the endless accumulation of yet-to-be-falsified statements that makes up scientific knowledge misses something deep as a result of a flaw in its fundamental orientation to the world.

Scientific reasoning works from the assumption that there is a knowing subject and an external world of objects. Taking this distinction as fundamental, it concentrates attention on the subjective image of the outer world and, by controlling experience through the construction of experiments and tests, seeks to refine that image by eliminating fallacies, misconceptions and falsehoods (these may originate in such things as deficiencies of reasoning, failures of language or lack of evidence). But what if the premise – of a discrete, knowing subject and an opaque object – is itself wrong? Critical theory prefers to start by acknowledging that the subject is itself a part of nature; that the boundary between it and the outer world has a history, was produced. This history is part biological, to be sure, but is also shot through with social and cultural events and transformations. The appearance of an epistemic subject is itself one of these events, and it is no coincidence that it emerged at the same historical point (in the seventeenth century) as the 'acquisitive individuals' of bourgeois political theory (MacPherson 1962).

For Adorno, there is a basic tension between the success of science, especially its privileged form of rationality – deductive logic – and our more fundamental, intuitive sense of the world and our place in it. This tension is most clearly manifest in the continued existence of art as a social institution, which long since ceased to be based on standards of accuracy in representation (if it ever was) and presents images and experiences that are constitutively resistant to logical analysis. Art is a revealing anomaly in a thoroughly rationalised world. For Adorno – and indeed something similar obtains in Heidegger's reflections on poetry (2014)[12] – its continued existence and the fact that humans still seem to need it is suggestive of a fundamental dislocation within the spirit of modern life. Adorno maintains that what people get from art is reflection on and reaction against enforced identity, the subject–object split at the heart of modern science and technology.

This relates to Marx's reflections on the experiential impoverishment of workers in capitalist society. In his 1844 manuscripts Marx bemoans the distorted development of the human senses, which become focused on owning things, while his later work highlights the brutalisation of human sensibilities in industrial labour. These developments have implications for the relationship of the species to the truth. Discerning a distinctive but largely implicit (unelaborated) epistemology here, Feenberg writes that Marx appears to be advocating 'a unique form of phenomenalism' (1981: 219). This is the basis upon which Feenberg advances an aesthetic dimension to his own critique of modernity and especially modern technology.

In Feenberg's work the critique of scientific or instrumental reason in the Frankfurt School becomes the wry observation that scientific laws are 'always subtly eccentric with respect to the real' (1981: 274). He maintains that the goal of revolutionary politics is to change society, 'in its most basic definition of reality, in its paradigm of rationality, in its founding practices' (1981: 196), and he even claims that, 'Marx founds a new concept of reason in revolution through an *ontological* treatment of *social* categories' (1981: 2–3; emphasis in original text). But even as he mines Marx for an implicit alternative epistemology, he redirects the efforts of critical theory away from a direct challenge to science or instrumental methods of analysis.

Feenberg also attempts to move beyond the principle of nonidentity as the ground of critique. His inspiration for this is Marcuse. In *One-Dimensional Man* (1964) Marcuse argues that, rather than having recourse to high art,[13] it is possible to envisage a more political response to the rationalised cultural conditions described by critical theory. Paradoxically, this might even be made possible by developments within the sphere of technology itself. Marcuse provides a glimpse of a less dystopian perspective on technology when he entertains the possibility that a new direction for technical development (1964: 227–229) might arise immanently to the sphere of technology design, resulting in technics guided by freely chosen human ends and informed by aesthetic values (1964: 239–240). He speculates that a new generation of technicians might create a less rationalised way of life not by renouncing technical reason but by putting a distinctive twist on it. The technics of the future might then comport with more liberated, experimental forms of social life. As Feenberg puts it, 'Marcuse elaborated a positive theory of liberated technical practice' (1981: 250).

Feenberg finds philosophical significance in Marcuse's vision, arguing that it shows that non-identity is merely a negative principle which says only that science as it is now is not the whole truth while interpreting art as the sign of an insuperable absence, namely the missing reconciliation of humans with inner and outer nature. In his early work, Feenberg argues that Marcuse envisaged something more positive, namely the active reconciliation of subject and object based on alternative technology:

> Here the Frankfurt School's insistence on non-identity is superseded by a different kind of identity, the identity of nature *in* subject and object, which recognises itself in reflection and aesthetic appreciation and mediates itself in a positing that affirms rather than transforms what is. (1981: 252)

This is an important passage because it highlights the fact that Feenberg skates close to the embrace of an ontological critique of capitalist modernity to be implemented, as it were, through a utopian technics of reconciliation. Critical theory's attachment to non-identity as the only residue of meaningful resistance is here replaced by an organicist holism that affirms nature as the common basis in reality of subject and object. In declaring that his theory warrants a consciousness that affirms rather than resists identity and seeks a new, higher unity to be established on alternative technical foundations, Feenberg also theorises a political space within technology design, rather than denouncing technology as simply the agent of instrumentalism. This is the space of technical politics.

While the influence of Marcuse is clear in this discussion, it would be quite wrong to read Feenberg as simply recycling the ideas of an earlier generation of theorists. In particular, while he retains a critical focus on modes of rationality and the entanglements of scientific discourse in questions of social power, his critique of technology does not involve the challenge to science, or the imputation of limits to the reach of science, that is common to Adorno and Heidegger. Feenberg detaches radical critique of technology from the question of whether science itself is biased. He writes that 'we need not await the reform of science to reform technological design' (2002: 28). This suggests that the nature he affirms in his vision of a future society is the same one that is studied by contemporary science. Feenberg is in this respect more philosophically conservative than earlier critical theorists but more politically radical: he drops the critique of identity-based epistemology but argues for the possibility of some kind of willed transformation of technology, which would be the solution to Marx's paradox.

3 Ambivalence

Feenberg's concept of ambivalence is intended to grasp the fact that the critical theory of technology sits between broad questions concerning the character of a civilisation and specific ones concerning how things get done. Culture, he says, is embedded in technology, which it needs to survive and to sustain itself as such, while technology is profoundly rooted in culture, from which it takes its challenges and problems. In this way, culture sets what he calls the horizon on technology while technology is a powerful determinant on social power relations within a culture. The web of dependencies here is central to Feenberg's dialectic, which can be represented diagrammatically as shown in Figure 1.

For Feenberg, the ambivalence of technology consists in the fact that on one side it is a feature of daily life and as such routinely modified, contested and argued over with regard to specific things that it does: solving or causing a problem, making a process more efficient, excluding some users, etc. On the other side, technology is closely bound up with the image people have of their society, even the civilisation of which they are members. The notions of 'post-industrial' or 'informational' society are used in a fairly routine way, for instance, and they suggest a mental map of the world that is coloured by a sense of technologies in their specific differences from others (this is explicit in the designation 'post-industrial', but implicit in the reference to IT, as against older machinery, in 'informational society').

Feenberg's argument is that in 'our modern society in which devices form a near total environment' (2002: 17), everyday activities with technology touch upon the meaning of civilisation itself. Technology is shaped and moulded by social actors with competing and sometimes conflicting demands. When technology changes and new artefacts come into use, this feeds back into practice, changing the actors along with their requirements and expectations. Each such iteration, or twist in the socio-technical entwinement reflects a modification to the meaning of

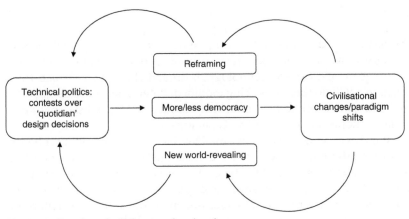

Figure 1 Feenberg's dialectic of technology

technology and, therefore, life itself. In a technical civilisation, or one that thinks of itself in those terms, these issues are mediated differently than in other societies.

The meaning of 'technology' in a society that has more mobile phones than humans is different than it was in one where most peoples' experience of devices was the machinery they operated in the factory where they worked.[14] Less obviously perhaps, this has implications for how people imagine the social world, including its possibilities, which Feenberg calls 'potential', and the limitations set by society on what counts as 'realistic'. A clear illustration of this point is the way that the use of social media has changed the meaning of 'society', raising hopes and fears in ways that scholars are still struggling to come to terms with.

There is a second dimension to Feenberg's dialectic, however, which goes beyond the reflexive implications of new technologies for the meanings of old concepts. His argument is that the principled basis of social disputes over the meanings of specific devices also affects the cultural practices internal to technology development. In industrial society, he says, technology developed in a way that was largely autonomous, beyond the control of day-to-day struggles and contests. Large corporations and government research institutes controlled how technology was developed, with no interruptions from interested parties, citizen activists or non-expert groups. The result was a society that was largely deferential to the authority of technology and to its associated experts. This technocratic system was the dystopian social image targeted by the earlier generation of critical theorists discussed in the previous section.

Feenberg's suggestion is that this part of the dialectic of technology development is changing. As people take a more active role in questioning technology design and even start to demand technologies that serve their interests rather than just those of powerful organisations and elites, so this has altered the way that they think about both technology and society. In this way, he says, the horizon on technology development – the kinds of things people expect technology to do and the ways in which they imagine it will do them – is being modified. Potentially, more democracy in the design of technology could bring about a wider, civilisational shift.

Iain Thomson, in his essay 'Feenberg's technical politics: between substantivism and constructivism', identifies a tension in Feenberg's theory at this point. He writes: 'the crucial question is: can ontic political decisions and resistance of the type Feenberg puts his faith in ever affect the kind of ontological change Heidegger seeks?' (in Veak 2006: 60). This question is central to any assessment of the success or failure of Feenberg's project, and therefore it is a central theme of the current work. Feenberg's view is that, viewed in ontic terms, modern technology is 'a human and environmental disaster' (2002: 9). 'Modern technology', he writes, 'embodies the values of a particular industrial civilization and especially those of elites that rest their claim to hegemony on technical mastery' (2002: v). However, he doesn't trace the negative impacts of technology to modern technology's 'essence', as Heidegger does, but rather to its place in an ensemble of social and political relations.[15]

The problems posed by technology are in many ways cataclysmic, which sometimes leads Feenberg to write as if his theory participated in Heideggerian paranoia about the loss of a world, but his understanding of these problems and of technology's role in them is consistently political, ontic rather than ontological. Feenberg is explicit in saying that this position gives him access to the polemical and other features of what is known as a 'substantivist' critique of technology while maintaining a strictly social constructivist position. On this basis he consistently advocates a politicised constructivism, within which democracy is presented as the solution. When dealing with the threats technology poses, he writes:

> The remedy is therefore not to be found in spiritual renewal but in a democratic advance. That advance implies a radical reconstruction of the technical basis of modern societies. (2002: 13–14)

Whether this argument succeeds depends in part on the extent to which Feenberg's reliance on characterising technology in terms of a distinctive rationality can really be distinguished from substantivist notions of enframing and a narrowing of worldview. It also turns on whether a constructivist, political grasp of technology as socially shaped can comprehend the kind of cultural and civilisational consequences that Feenberg's critical theory highlights and purports to offer a way of changing. Finally, it depends crucially on whether democratisation and what he calls 're-aestheticisation' in the sphere of technology design can bear the large historical weight – of accounting for civilisational change – that Feenberg chooses to rest on them. These questions are central to the discussion that follows in later chapters of this book.

4 Technical reason

Feenberg sometimes freights technology with the kind of negative significance assigned to it by earlier critical theorists and 'substantivist' philosophers of technology. At the same time, though, he maintains that the central concepts in his version of this negative characterisation are in fact ambivalent and reflect social determination, not conditioning by an unchanging essence of technology. This preserves a space in which technology might be contested and its design altered so as to facilitate a different kind of technical civilisation.

To clarify this, he introduces a key distinction between technical reason, which is present in any instance of technology regardless of context, and what he calls 'technological rationality', which is specific to capitalist modernity and indeed hegemonic in that social formation. The thoroughgoing imbrication of these two – indeed, they are inseparable in practice – is what led the earlier generation of thinkers to view technology as irretrievably implicated in the dark side of modernity. In contrast, Feenberg maintains that technical reason might be liberated from its current entanglement in the socially dominant form of rationality and occupy a more benign place in an alternative constellation.

Calling technological rationality 'hegemonic' means that it is the dominant way of doing things and that it is so because it is perceived as objectively the right and 'neutral' way to solve problems. It is as a manifestation of technological rationality that technology is authoritative.[16] Technology as such is produced and sustained (in use) through a reciprocal interplay of technical solutions (devices and designs that work) and the prevailing conception of technology (as authoritative). There is circularity here: because technology 'works' it is seen as beyond question, and because it is authoritative it gets introduced into more situations, where it works.

Constructivist scholars have demonstrated that the idea of technology 'working' is not as straightforward as it might seem. Their fables, which usually describe the early development of specific technologies, demonstrate that the pattern in technology development is not the common sense one of a problem encountered and solved by a designed solution. Much more often, technology gets introduced to a pre-existing situation with a degree of indeterminacy about what it is 'for'. Once it starts to operate then people discover how it 'works', in the sense that they learn how to operate it but also in the more surprising one that they learn its capabilities and advantages and then restructure their practices around it, to extract some unanticipated (or barely glimpsed) benefit. As Feenberg puts it, 'clarity on these matters is often the outcome rather than the pre-supposition of technical development' (2001: 79). A very clear illustration of this would be the home or personal computer of the 1980s, which, as Feenberg points out, was 'launched on the market with infinite promise and no applications' (2001: 85).

Technology, then, always appears to be the 'obvious solution' once it is present in a situation, and this is a key part of its peculiar authority. Machinery enters the workplace and is accepted because it is machinery – in Feenberg's terms, it is 'codified' as such. Luddism – refusing to accept technology, or resisting the machines – has become the very paradigm of irrationality or eccentricity. Technological rationality is a codification of technical artefacts, which ensures that once they are in place in a given situation they reproduce the dominant structure of power. Technology both destabilises prior arrangements, since it imposes a change in what people do, and re-enforces social power relations to ensure that the new situation that emerges reproduces and extends the hold of dominant interests.

This seems very one-sided for a theory of ambivalence, but Feenberg's metaphor of codification brings something to the situation that is absent when technology is conceived only as a mode of rationality, or ontologic-ally as enframing the world. Codes are flexible: they can be interpreted and reinterpreted, and they can be turned around and used to make new programs, or 'inscriptions'.[17] If technical reason, the efficacious core of any given technology, is the key stake in the game, conditioning its employ-ment and use, the moves in this game concern the details of design – that is, how that core of capabilities gets articulated to practical purposes, serving specific social interests in concrete situations. The meaning of ambivalence, therefore, is that while technology always advances social domination, it also tends to proliferate openings for people to exploit, through which they can resist power and extract unintended benefits for themselves.

Feenberg does not conceive reformed technology in terms of a different world-revealing, which would be the ontological conception of civilisation change, but rather anticipates that multiple, local contests for control over the meanings of different technological capacities will add up to a shift in the meaning of technology as a whole. Such a change would of necessity be part of a wider change to the way that people con-ceive the social world and their place in it, and, as discussed above, for Feenberg technology would be central to this. As part of this transform-ation, technology might lose its authoritative character and its asso-ciation with dominant social interests, though this is not a possibility Feenberg ever entertains. Taken together, these changes might herald what substantivists would understand as an alternative world-revealing, but, unlike his critical theory forebears, Feenberg is not focused on this aspect and it is not one of his objectives to set out a theory that comprehends civilisation change in those terms.

One strength of his theory is precisely that it considers technology and the question of technology design independently of ideas about science. Treating technology as autonomous of science saves Feenberg from the charge of prevarication between substantivism and constructivism. His disavowal of the critique of physical and natural sciences, which contrasts with his view of the human sciences,[18] means that the question of alternative modes of world-revealing is, at the very least, deferred. Technology reform may ultimately issue in a change of civilisational paradigm, but the implications of this for how humans relate to and understand nature are a function of technical politics and not the other way around. In this sense Feenberg is firmly on the side of constructivists, who limit their analyses to accounts of proximal factors shaping this or that individual technology design. His focus is not on deepening such accounts in the direction of their implications for ontology but rather in broadening them to include an account of their political significance.

As stated in the Introduction, Feenberg's engagement with constructivism was decisive in the development of his theory. Constructivist scholars provide detailed historical accounts of the social shaping of technical artefacts. They show how the competing interests of different social actors at the scene of invention and in the various phases of product development are manifest in (sometimes opposed or conflicting) descriptions. These latter are more or less determinate in their consequences for the resulting artefacts, depending on the support they get from wider social constituencies. For some people, bicycles were 'safety' bicycles, while others sought the more excitingly named 'bone shakers', and it was a social conflict or competition between these social groups that finally shaped the modern bike, rather than any narrow technical considerations (Bijker et al 1989).

A widely acknowledged failing of constructivist work is that while these narratives disclose the importance of social actions and actors in making technologies what they are, they do so largely in abstraction from questions of social power or politics (Winner 1993). Constructivist studies in STS effectively relativise the whole question of what technology is to its social co-ordinates, highlighting the role of motivated human choices above all other factors in the shaping of artefacts. The focus is on a specific 'semiotic hinge' (Bijker 1997: 197), where words and meanings from limited practical contexts get folded into the specifications for a 'good' tool. This is a strangely decontextualised approach to language and design communities, which almost always brackets out wider sociological questions about the class background of participants and historical ones regarding the wider cultural context and how its meanings limit and condition more proximal actors' choices.

However, for Feenberg, constructivism puts a helpful spotlight on the role of human agency in technology design. Technology is not determined by science or by standards that are technical 'in-themselves'. Rather, constructivists show that technical choices are 'underdetermined' by such considerations: whenever any two technologists disagree over a design decision then social factors are in play. The constructivist scholar pores over diaries and notebooks to identify what they were and to chart the social 'causes' that inform each step (e.g. Bijker 1997). But while they identify 'the social' as the shaping force, they tend to overlook *its* contradictory and conflicted nature, with the result that their narratives, while sometimes replete with surprising insights pertinent to the history of specific artefacts, lack critical force or purchase on the wider entanglements of technological designs.

Feenberg agrees with the basic constructivist insight that 'many paths lead out from the first forms of a new technology' and that 'there are always viable technical alternatives that might have been developed in place of the successful one' (2001: 10). However, he politicises constructivism by observing that the social context itself contains contradictions and that, beyond the narrow set of group-specific rival interpretations that tend to manifest in laboratory disputes, social power is a factor in overdetermining design. On this basis, Feenberg concludes that 'The evolution of technology can no longer be regarded as an autonomous process but must be rooted in interests and social forces' (2002: 49). His main innovation in relation to constructivism consists in his understanding of those forces in terms of a theory of their historical and political significance.

By articulating the constructivist insight that the notion of 'working' technology is a product of multiple social determinations to the Marxian critique of technology design as shaped by class interests, Feenberg radically alters the significance of constructivism. The point then becomes not that inefficient technology might be 'equally as good' as efficient technology, whatever that might mean, but that efficiency itself is a socially contested notion, and one that is an important stake in many of the wider social disputes that shape technology development.

Feenberg (2003) explains what he means by this in an analysis of exploding boilers on nineteenth-century steamships. Company owners favoured boilers made with thinner outer skins because, using less metal, they were cheaper to make. However, these boilers were dangerous, as they tended to explode when pressure levels were high for extended periods of time. The explosions killed workers and cost the company money. Overall, though, in the eyes of the companies it was more efficient to continue using exploding boilers than to spend the extra money on safe ones. From their point of view, efficiency equated to short-term profitability.

Trades unions countered the idea that exploding boilers were best not by demanding less efficient machinery but by insisting that not blowing up workers should be part of the meaning of 'efficiency': machinery that occasionally kills its operatives cannot be considered efficient, even if it is more profitable.

Using this and other examples, Feenberg extends the constructivist insight that technology is technically underdetermined into controversies and discussions that are inherently political, rather than merely generating intriguing little tales that narrate the emergence of this or that device. In this way constructivism becomes a methodological first principle for technical politics. Feenberg argues that in recent decades there has been increased willingness among widening groups of people to engage in disputes about how technology should be used, including what the best and most efficient employment of it might be. Constructivism shows how social processes like this can alter technology design, focusing particularly on how rival social groups use language to shape technology to their ends by advancing descriptions that reflect the interest they take in it. This corresponds to Feenberg's notion of a technical code that can be reworked.

To develop the idea that disputes over the way technology is described should be understood as a struggle for control of its code, Feenberg draws on Michel Foucault's theory of discourse. Foucault's studies of madness (1985) and medicine (1986) showed that bodies of scientific knowledge are both reliable representations of social reality and inscribed in practices that produce the world they describe. Psychiatry is both objective knowledge regarding mental illness and, as discourse, itself an objective structure that works through institutions and practices to sort the world into fixed categorical orderings (sane/insane; well/unwell). These categories are both true, in the sense that phenomena are pulled together under them in a way that 'works', and shot through with social power: the insane and the sick are silenced and assigned a passive place within the institutional order while experts are given rights and entitlements to dispose over them.

Viewing technology as a mode of discourse enables Feenberg to extend the application of Foucault's thesis of an intimate alignment of knowledge and power. His argument casts technology as a structural component of modern societies aligned to the aforementioned discourses and practices. Like language, or discourse, technology is a material force in the world and an agent of the imposition of a particular rationality. Coming to terms with this, as the example of Luddism shows, involves internalising certain norms and complying with the rules that flow from them – not breaking the machines, following the instructions, etc. This reckoning with the authority of the machine is part of becoming a normalised subject rather than a deviant one. As Feenberg puts it, 'the condensation of social and technical determinations tends more and more to appear as the very definition of rationality' (2002: 67).

According to Foucault, reason itself is produced through these discursive codifications: rational subjects are defined by their avoidance of behaviour that has been labelled 'mad'. Being rational does not entail adherence to the rigorous procedures of logic – 'mad' people are often quite good at that – it means having the code work its way through one's body to produce a particular kind of interface with the wider social world. Those whose bodies do not accept the code find themselves on the wrong side of the lines drawn by discourse and become objects rather than subjects of discourse. As such they are effectively deprived of language as a resource for making sense of experience. Foucault's avowed aim in his famous book about madness was to reinscribe 'mad' people's experience in the historical record and in this sense to let unreason speak.

Some Foucault scholarship has highlighted the similarity between his thought and that of Heidegger (Eribon 2011: 85; Han 1998: 12). Both identify objective scientific-technical institutions and structures with a particular worldview that is associated with domination. For Foucault this is the modern episteme; for Heidegger it is Western metaphysics. Both thinkers highlight the role of reason and rationality as promoting a practice of sense-making that is exclusionary: Foucault writes of the 'rarefaction' of discourse (Foucault 1981: 58), the way that it excludes prohibited, illicit formulations and ways of speaking about and interacting with the world that are considered unacceptable by power. Similarly, perhaps, Heidegger writes that the essence of modern technology is nothing technological but is rather a 'world-revealing' that only discloses raw material to be used, excluding other ways of being.

Feenberg draws on Foucault, however, primarily as a critical theorist of rationality.[19] His interest is not in highlighting an 'other' of technological reason which might correspond to the utopian technologies of the future, but rather in another aspect of Foucault's critique, namely his thesis that there is no power without resistance. Whereas Heidegger's critique of modern rationality leads to a search for poetic language to articulate the fundamental homelessness of modern humans in a world fashioned by instrumental reason and domination, Foucault shows that the order of discourse can only produce a normalised subject because it (discourse) always encounters resistance. No one is completely normal: everyone dabbles in madness, often positively framing it as 'character' or 'personality'. In the interstices of a legislated normality the more fundamental condition is strangeness, difference.[20]

Feenberg argues that such difference tends also to emerge in human relations with technology. This means that, viewed as the inscription of the correct way to use any given device, the technical code is only efficacious because it runs up against a buffer, namely the human element. This element is, of course, compliant; the program compiles and runs in the sense that human beings use the technology effectively. At the same time, however, they resist, not by smashing the machines (they aren't 'insane') but by exploring possibilities and capacities within the devices. Gamers modify game code, for example, to unlock or even to create 'cheats', patients' groups circumvent safety regimes to claim an active role in drug trials, unemployed people use hacked software to game government 'job-seeking systems' and so on.

Drawing on Michel de Certeau's (1984) distinction between strategy and tactics, Feenberg writes that the strategic standpoint of managers implementing technology 'privileges considerations of control and efficiency' (2002: 16), while the tactical standpoint of the managed is 'far richer'. Tactical operations on the part of multitudinous subjects are grounded in the 'everyday life-world of a modern society in which devices form a nearly total environment' (2002: 17) and create openings in technology design. These diverse, widely diffuse practices of resistance centred on the contextual meanings of technology are challenges to the authority of technologists, managers and technology itself. For Feenberg they add an indispensable dimension to the extension of democracy envisaged in the Marxist critique of capitalism.

5 Technology and socialist transition

When Feenberg writes that 'under socialism, workers ... can change the very nature of technology' (2002: 53), he envisages not a wholesale, all-at-once transformation in what we mean by 'technology' but rather a series of changes to tool and machinery design which, taken in aggregate, will amount to a drastic overhaul of the material infrastructure of society and of the human relationship to that infrastructure and the world beyond it. Under socialism, thinking technically will carry with it a set of different connotations than those that come to mind at present. If capitalist technology symbolises efficiency, authority and enhanced control, socialist techniques will be disposed towards the solving of human problems, greater care for the environment and the qualitative enhancement of human experience. Feenberg's vision is firmly focused on political change and the place of technology in securing and implementing that change, with the issue of fundamental world-relations, including a less instrumental relationship with nature, a more distant concern.

Feenberg upholds the constructivist principle that technology is only as it is codified and not anything 'in-itself'. Hence, the codification can be changed, pushing technology into new forms and, potentially at least, a different place in the social imaginary. As part of this development, the material reality of technology will be affected so that designs will bear the impress of a different cultural reality, and this in turn will alter the prevailing idea of what technology is or can be, and of what natural reality is like and how it should be approached. This way of construing things frustrates Thomson and leads him, in the above-mentioned critical essay, to view Feenberg as caught between essentialism and constructivism. Thomson's critique misses the mark, but it highlights the problem that politics is a multi-layered practice operative across more than one temporal register. Workplace arguments over the most efficient use of e-mail, for example, are at several steps' remove from more long-standing conventions and codifications that condition what technology is and can be. At times, in his development of technical politics, Feenberg conflates these two levels of analysis.

This enables him to suggest that principled interventions in technology design – in favour of designs that broaden participation, against those that deskill or dehumanise workers, for instance – obviously comport with a wider shift in the technological imaginary, or the place people assign to technology in their mental model of society. This is an intriguing claim, on which much else in Feenberg's theory rests, but it also raises many questions, which, as we will see later, he doesn't address. It must be acknowledged that there is a kind of evasion here when it comes to discussing and classifying actual technologies in terms of the political dramaturgy that underpins Feenberg's thesis. How much of the discussion around any given technology is susceptible to analysis in terms of its democratic or aesthetic principles? Moreover, the notion that functioning artefacts are thoroughly shaped by such concerns seems to assume that they (the artefacts) have nothing to say about their role in the situations in which they operate.

Feenberg envisages a technical politics in which people enthuse about and participate in technologies and technical decisions without direct reference to wider ontological issues. His conviction is that in making design more democratic and in opening it up to aesthetic values that humanise technology, it will be improved. Feenberg writes that in a socialist society, 'reconstruction would not be determined by immanent laws of technological development but on the contrary by social and political choices' (2002: 51). His argument is that these choices can be determinate for technology design and that the outcome of democratic design will be a change of civilisational model. The idea of technical politics connects these two things and is what enables Feenberg to evade the charge of prevarication levelled at him by Thomson. Feenberg is determinedly not an essentialist, but whether he succeeds in building a bridge between the ontic and ontological levels depends on your assessment of the overall success of his theory.

The vision of broad societal transformation effected by politicised technology development is informed by the affirmative principle that a better world is possible and the belief that technology design is an important, perhaps the most important, part of how that world can be created. This attitude includes openness to, perhaps even faith in, the idea of a technological event that might produce the kind of global perspective shift required to take us into a new civilisation. There is, though, no account in Feenberg's theory of how such an event might be willed into existence. Feenberg is not asking us to start imagining new technologies for a new world. The technology he affirms is the technology that is here now, among us. His theory reflects the fact that people seem to be engaging with that, arguing about it and changing it in ways that were unthinkable just a few decades ago. There is no 'essence' of technology to contend with and, even if there were, his technical politics does not go there. Technical politics involves challenging bias in existing technology designs. Feenberg's theory targets the underlying logics that produce such bias and identifies openings for the development of alternative design principles, including aesthetic values, which might inform the development of an alternative technology for a better civilisation. These themes are the focus of the next four chapters.

Notes

1 They write that 'today machinery disables men even as it nurtures them' (Adorno and Horkheimer 1997: 37).
2 Marx writes, for example, that the dreadful conditions in nineteenth-century garment factories were 'nurtured by the very nature of the sewing machine' and says that the 'fearful increase in death from starvation during the past ten years in London runs in parallel with the extension of machine sewing' (1990: 601, 603).
3 There is disagreement in the literature over the ways in which this might matter. For those who focus on Marx's later writings, the diminution of the quality of the labour process under capitalism will be offset by a reduction in the quantity of labour undertaken in socialism. Everyone will have to do a little bit of unpleasant work, but the real focus of life will be leisure time. For interpreters who are more influenced by Marx's early works, especially the 1844 *Manuscripts*, the realm of 'all-round development' entails a qualitative shift in the character of work so that it becomes, as Marx put it in one of his later texts, 'life's prime want' (1978: 18). It is obviously harder to reconcile that view with the notion that communism inherits its technical foundation from capitalism.
4 Marx writes that 'the field of application for machinery would ... be entirely different in a communist society from what it is in bourgeois society' (1990: 515 fn 33).
5 Hysteresis is, or can be, a feature of functional explanations. Cohen (1978) and Elster (1986) discuss the implications of this for social explanation, reaching opposed conclusions.

6 Marx's failure to address the question is largely reproduced in recent scholarly literature. For example, David Harvey, in his commentary on *Capital*, touches on the paradox discussed here but then defers serious reflection on it, writing only that 'a socialist revolutionary project *in the long term* cannot … avoid the question of the definition of an alternative technological basis' (2010: 219; my emphasis).

7 The abolition of private property would lead to the 'emancipation of all human senses and qualities', presumably meaning that the world would feel different to liberated humans (1981: 94).

8 This designation is not, of course, original to Feenberg – but he gives it a new priority, as will be explored further in the next chapter.

9 For Lukàcs, the solution lies in revolutionary praxis oriented to breaking down the twin illusions of the vivacity of things and the passivity of people in the process of building a revolutionary party.

10 Applied to technology, Lukàcs's concept of reification bears strong resemblance to Martin Heidegger's notion of enframing. As Lucien Goldmann pointed out (1977), Lukàcs formulated his ideas some decades earlier and was almost certainly an unacknowledged influence on Heidegger's thinking.

11 One of the aims of the current book is to correct Feenberg's pro-Marcuse bias and to show that on certain key points Adorno is a more useful ally to the critical theory of technology.

12 Heidegger (2013, chapter 1) targets a sense that something is missing from modern experience which can be addressed not directly from within that experience but only allusively, using poetic language. The continued hold of poetry on moderns, who are taught from a young age to favour practical and effective modes of action, speaks to the sense of something profound being overlooked.

13 According to Adorno and Horkheimer, 'With the progress of Enlightenment, only authentic works of art were able to avoid the mere imitation of that which already is' (1997: 18) – that is, to escape the logic of equivalence and exchange.

14 Feenberg refers to 'an earlier consensus' that 'brooked no interference with the decisions of technical experts' and contrasts this with the 'increasing weight of pubic actors in technological development' (2002: 24). The latter seems to occur with the rise of digital technologies but is not limited to them in its effects.

15 'Substantive theory identifies the values embodied in current designs with the essence of technology as such … By contrast, the design critique relates the values embodied in technology to a social hegemony' (Feenberg 2002: 64).

16 Identifying the authoritative character of technology with its purported rationality is now so ingrained in the Marxist tradition as to be almost a habit. For example, Gregory Claeys, in his introduction to Marx and Marxism, suggests that, for Marx, 'technological rationality seemingly defines the limits of political will' (2018: 211), yet the phrase never appears in any of Marx's texts.

17 There is a parallel here with feminist theorists Dona Haraway (1991) and N. Katherine Hayles (1999), who also contrast the incorporation of technology, which involves submission and habituation to its behavioural templates, with

inscription, which is a process of refashioning, rewriting the tool – quite literally, in the age of programmable devices and platforms. Like Feenberg, they identify positive political potential in these practices of inscription.

18 In this respect Feenberg's critique resembles that of Michel Foucault, who also contrives to place the hard sciences outside the purview of his critique of epistemology (for discussion, see Eribon 2011: 358–370).

19 Feenberg is quite selective in his use of Foucault's ideas. It is worth noting that the latter rejected a strong association of his approach with that of critical theory, saying: 'I don't think that the Frankfurt School can accept that what we need to do is not recover our lost identity, or liberate our imprisoned nature, or discover our fundamental truth; rather, it is to move towards something altogether different' (2002: 275). This remark applies equally well to Feenberg's project of redeeming technology by way of progressive rationalization articulated through democratic technical politics.

20 The priority of the pathological over the healthy was explored by Foucault's mentor George Canguilheim (2007).

2

The theory of bias and the ethics of technology design

This chapter focuses on Feenberg's development of a theory of bias in technology designs. The idea of bias is central to his overall project of developing a critical theory of technology, since it explains the entanglement of technology in issues of social power and domination. Feenberg argues that technology in modern societies is 'formally biased' and uses this idea to identify technology design as a field that is thoroughly political yet rarely recognised or theorised as such. The notion of formal bias establishes a space for critical and ethical concerns within technology and technology studies.

Like other critical theorists, Feenberg presents a philosophical argument whose viability rests crucially on philosophy's inclusion in its own discourse of insights from other scholarly disciplines, especially the study of politics and society. At the same time, the argument is intended to open a route for philosophy to 'speak' to other disciplines as well – in particular, to cast a critical light on contingent features of social reality that those disciplines study 'up close', so to speak.[1] In the case of critical theory of technology, if it is to be anything more than a scholastic reflection on technology's relation to society, Feenberg's philosophy must connect with disciplines that study and participate in technology design.

Feenberg presents the idea of bias as a way to clarify issues of social fairness at stake in technology design because it enables critical theory to engage with and mediate ideas from technical and other disciplines while decisively liberating the theory from its essentialist heritage. Drawing on social theory rather than philosophy, Feenberg aligns the 'neutral' appearance of technology with Max Weber's thesis that modern societies are characterised by 'rationalisation'. Technology is viewed both as an agent in that process and as being itself shaped by it, which is why it appears to be both rational (neutral) and a factor in alienation and the loss of meaning associated with cultural modernity.

In this chapter, I argue that the concept of bias is more useful when detached from the theme of societal rationalisation and deployed instead as the conceptual route towards a technology design ethics. Bias in technology design is better understood without invoking different modes of rationality, which are too broad to afford a secure grip on contemporary social phenomena. Instead, philosophical concerns can gain a foothold in technical politics by identifying normative principles immanent to design practice, understood as a special kind of communicative process.

Section 1 describes Feenberg's preferred account of modernity and its relationship to rationalisation. This section shows how, rejecting the option of an essentialist critique of technology, Feenberg clears the way for a strictly contextual understanding of bias in technology design. It presents his argument that in capitalist societies technology can both be formally neutral – that is, not obviously designed to be unfair – and yet function to produce and reinforce social injustices. Feenberg explains this, the formal bias of capitalist technology, with reference to the uniquely formal character of rationality in modern societies, which he says skews contemporary technology design. This section identifies a tension or discrepancy between Feenberg's emphasis on the problematic character of abstract 'formal reason' and his focus on concrete instances of bias in technology, of the kind that concerned Marx.

The next two sections present a detailed analysis of the concept of formal bias, concentrating particularly on Feenberg's presentation of the concept in his (2010) *Between Reason and Experience*. There he suggests that there may be several versions of formal bias and focuses on two of them, which he calls 'constitutive' and 'implementation' bias. Subjecting this argument to critical scrutiny, Section 2 argues that the distinction requires further clarification. In particular, there appears to be some overlap between constitutive formal bias and the kind of substantive design bias Feenberg says he rejects.

The discussion then moves to the test implied by Feenberg's discussion for the presence of formal bias in technology design. This turns on two features of the situation, namely (1) the nature of the intention through which technology comes to bear the impress of social determinations, and (2) the sociologically understood consequences of the design in practice. The formal bias of capitalist technology involves a distinctively 'neutral', or value-free, consciousness on the part of technologists that is focused on efficiency gains. Paradoxically, this is what generates biased designs that systematically favour one social group. Technology is formally biased only in context, and the outcomes generated by a technology design are contingent features that emerge when the technology is operational in a specific social setting. Of particular importance here are outcomes that favour the reproduction of what Feenberg calls the 'operational autonomy' of managers and owners in the economy.

Formal bias is present when neutral intentions at the scene of design are conjoined with the socially regressive enlargement of operational autonomy for favoured groups. Section 3 highlights the existence of cases that are problematic for this theory and clarifies the ambiguity concerning constitutive formal bias. The purpose of this argument is to rehabilitate a version of substantive bias but without opening a door to Feenberg's Heideggerian and conservative critics, whose substantivism consists in maintaining there is something *essentially malign* about modern technology. Instead, it becomes clear that substantive technical bias is a meaningful category because bias is a property of all technology, even though the precise nature of this bias can only ever be specified in social context. The point is that technology designs are biased – that is, they are substantively inclined to favour some interests over others – even when they do not fit either of Feenberg's definitions (constitutive or implementation) of formal bias. These technologies are sociologically significant in their effects, and their problematic nature arises from their technological character (they present issues that rarely arise in connection with other classes of object).

Feenberg's critics have misread his comments on substantivist critique of technology as reflecting an indecision on the question of the transhistorical nature of technology as something opposed to the human. His alignment of formal rationality with technical reason as a definitive property of modern technology reinforces this impression, but, nonetheless, the critics are wrong – Feenberg's true definition is thoroughly historical and relational. His point is that formal rationality biases technology design as a matter of contingent historical fact. The confusion, I submit, partially stems from the fact that this contingency has itself shifted, or ceased to obtain, so that technical bias is no longer well understood with reference to competing forms of rationality, especially not the opposition of technical or instrumental reason to communicative or other kinds. Feenberg's real point, which is that technology is always biased in context and not in virtue of some inhuman or anti-human essence, stands.

Here it is useful to supplement Feenberg's argument with ideas from post-phenomenological philosophies of technology, which emphasise the role of technical artefacts as agents or quasi-subjects rather than more or less inert objects. Feenberg's attempts to comprehend this are impeded by his framing of technology in terms of its association with a distinctive kind of societal rationality. Detached from a rationalisation-based historical perspective, technical politics becomes more messy and requires more diverse tactics than a battle between two opposed forms of reasoning. To illustrate this, I present examples of substantively biased technologies that ought to be subject to a strategy of containment – that is, considered unacceptable by critical theorists on terms that are immanent to design as a social practice. Section 4 considers Feenberg's objections to containment of technology development and argues that they do not apply to these cases.

In concluding, I make the connection between desirable kinds of containment and Jürgen Habermas's idea of discourse ethics. Just as some discursive acts are ruled impermissible because they could not, in principle, be assented to by all participants in a given debate, so I argue that some technologies ought to be disbarred on similar grounds, and that this standpoint can be useful in developing the idea of design bias in the direction of an immanent ethics. The latter ought to form a supplement to Feenberg's project of democratic technical politics. A sociologically informed ethical critique at the scene of design is one of Feenberg's objectives, and clarifying the nature of technology's bias is an important step towards its fulfilment. The argument of this chapter suggests that his attachment to broad, historically grounded rationality concepts obscures relevant sociological details and inhibits Feenberg's successful pursuit of this goal, even though his introjection of social elements into the philosophical definition of technology makes it possible.

1 Varieties of bias

Feenberg views technology as a fundamental institution of modernity and as a fundamentally modern institution. Making the case for bringing modernity theory into discussions of technology, he asks rhetorically, 'how can one expect to understand modernity without an adequate account of the technological developments that make it possible, and how can one study specific technologies without a theory of the larger society in which they develop?' (in Misa *et al* 2003: 73). Technology is distinctive in modern societies because it bears the imprint of the capitalist and bureaucratic context associated with modernity. At the same time, technology is a catalyst or relay that amplifies some of the core tendencies of cultural modernity, so in this sense they work together. Technical systems work with causal propensities in the natural world by steering known physical regularities to achieve human ends, and, as such, they are inherently rule-bound. This imbrication with rules is particularly pronounced in modernity, and that is part cause, part effect, of technology's relationship to other institutions in modern societies.

Modern technology presents as neutral, objective and obvious, so that to reject it is to be perceived as foolish, anachronistic or worse. Similarly, the institutions of modernity present themselves as formally neutral in the sense that their behaviour is controlled by rules that have three defining properties. They are transparent, which means that anyone who accesses a given system can, in principle at least, find out what the rules are and use the system accordingly. They are universal in their application, so that everyone is equally subject to the rules without exceptions based on social status or individual identity. Finally, the rules that constitute modern organisations are enforced in a manner that is separate from the issue of their purpose or that of the organisation of which they are part. This often creates the feeling that the rules get between people and whatever service they expect an organisation to provide. However, whether a modern institution works or not is a matter of its processes and the extent to which these are well ordered and efficient. The goals of the organisation are separate from the question of its performance.

The fact of being based on these kinds of rules is part of what differentiates modern from pre-modern institutions. In Britain before the reforms of the 1820s, for example, and for some time after them, law and its enforcement were inconsistent across the country. A local lord or bishop often had the authority to determine punishments and could vary them almost at will depending on their view of the plaintiff as well as their crime (Reiner 2000). The projects of standardising and publicising law are in large measure constitutive of the modernity of modern societies. Immanuel Kant placed particular importance on the publicity criterion as essential to legitimacy in law, writing that no 'actions affecting the rights of other human beings' could be valid if 'their maxim is not compatible with their being made public' (1992: 126). All modern political philosophy shares the conviction that systems are only fair if they apply equally to all and are objective in the sense entailed by the three-point definition of modern rule systems given above. Only such systems are untainted by direct, substantive sectional interests and, in this way, they achieve the appearance of neutrality. They are neutral and unbiased in the sense that they explicitly identify their correct functioning in terms of serving a *general* social interest.

Max Weber (1974) argued that the spread of such standardised, rule-governed systems constituted 'societal rationalization'. He exposed a kind of circularity at the heart of modern, rationalised social structures. Describing the 'spirit of modern capitalism', as, 'that attitude which seeks profit rationally and systematically', for example, Weber says that this 'attitude has on one hand found its most suitable expression in capitalistic enterprise, while on the other the enterprise has derived its most suitable motive force from the spirit of capitalism' (1974: 65). This relates to the third point above, about organisations' distance from the ends or values they are supposed to serve. As modern societies develop increasingly sophisticated methods for measuring performance independent of content, so their institutions tend to erode their own reasons for existing in the first place. Building on Weber, other thinkers in the critical theory tradition, most notably Adorno and Horkheimer (1997), argue that while ideology, especially religion, had served to legitimise domination in pre-modern societies, in modern, bureaucratically administered societies this function increasingly passed to science and technology, where it was justified with reference to efficiency.

In *The Dialectic of Enlightenment* (1997), Adorno and Horkheimer suggest that in what they called the 'totally administered society', the contradictions of capitalism were cancelled by being managed through strategies of knowing manipulation that secure a culture of compliant consumerism. At the heart of this social system is identity-thinking – the principle that things can be grasped quantitatively and thereby brought under technical control. Modern science only sees the measurable world that it assumes is there in the first place, excluding from view nature's manifold qualitative aspects or considering them only as secondary. Modern culture extends this perspective to human beings and society, so that people are viewed as producers and/or consumers, their individual idiosyncrasies seen as problems to be handled by the system. This stark characterisation culminates in Marcuse's (1964) description of industrial modernity as a 'one-dimensional society'.

What Feenberg presents as 'modernity theory' is a synthesis of ideas from these and other sources concerned with the inner connection between increased differentiation of social capabilities achieved by modern institutions and the deleterious consequences of a socially diffuse emphasis on instrumental efficiency. In his reading of Weber, Feenberg contrasts the formal rationality characteristic of modern social systems with what he calls the substantive rationality of pre-modern societies:

> Rationality is substantive to the extent that it realizes a specific value such as feeding a population, winning a war, or maintaining the social hierarchy. The 'formal' rationality of capitalism refers to those economic arrangements which optimize calculability and control. Formally rational systems lie under technical norms that have to do with the efficiency of means rather than the choice of ends. (1991: 68)

Feenberg views the question of how technology, which seems to be the embodiment of a neutral, scientific understanding of the world in tools that work for human ends, can be biased, through the prism of its relationship to this formal rationality. Viewed in this way, technology is entangled in the Weberian tendency of modern societies to erode cultural values in the pursuit of efficient procedures. Importantly, however, this is not inherent to technology but something it acquires under the unique cultural conditions of modernity. Feenberg writes:

> The technical ideas combined in technology are neutral, but the study of any specific technology can trace in it the impress of a mesh of social determinations which preconstruct a whole domain of social activity aimed at definite goals. (1991: 81)

Feenberg here distinguishes between technology, the social context that shapes it and the consequences of that shaping in generating merely technical definitions of social situations and problems. Technology is shaped by capitalism, and this is what makes it biased in favour of the class interests of the bourgeoisie. However, this bias is not one that can be grasped in terms of deliberate, intentionally discriminatory warping of the substantive design of technology. That would produce machines materially adapted to serve some users' interests while making life harder and less pleasant for others, and created because they had those effects. Rather, the bias of technology design rests upon its increasingly formal character. It is in its appearance as neutral, as the self-evident solution to a problem, that technology is in fact biased to serve some social interests rather than others.[2]

This might make it seem as if radical or democratic critique ought to reclaim a stake in what Feenberg calls substantive rationality and allow this to fashion a new technology or, indeed, to resist technology as the source of an alienating way of approaching the world. That is the preferred solution of thinkers like Albert Borgmann (1984), who denounces what he calls the modern 'device paradigm' as sustaining a false way of being and opposes to it other 'focal' cultural practices that enable people to resuscitate meaning and restore values to the centre of social existence. Borgmann writes, for example, of a 'historic decline in meaning' associated with the development of modern computing (1999: 15). A 'focal' practice is one that involves a relationship to some part of the world that is sufficiently rich and subtle that it definitively evades capture in any quantitative rubric (Borgmann 1984: 81). Borgmann gives the example of running, a practice that for him has meditative, even spiritual benefits.

However, as seen in the previous chapter, part of Feenberg's project is to distance critical theory from substantivist conceptions which maintain technology has a negative essence that might cause it to be biased in the sense that it always impacts negatively upon human culture, and, as a result, steers modern societies towards various kinds of catastrophe. He argues that substantivist theory tends to confuse the lack of values in modern technology design with the essence of technology as such (Feenberg 1991: 66). Feenberg wants to focus critique instead on the social factors that make technology biased, which also involves distancing his theory from the critique of science implicit in Adorno and Horkheimer's denunciation of identity-thinking.

What Feenberg rejects in the idea that technology might be substantively biased is the notion that the technological as such is held to be inimical to certain interests, cultural practices or social groups. Instead, he insists that all of technology's bias, all the ways in which it prefers some groups over others or implements contentious values, only arise when the impress of social determinations at the scene of design is conjoined to specific social contexts of implementation. Hence, he writes that when Jacques Ellul (1964) and Martin Heidegger (1987) present all technology as incorrigibly instrumental, they confound 'the essence of technology with the hegemonic code that shapes its contemporary forms' (Feenberg 1991: 181).

Feenberg's attitude to substantivist arguments like theirs, which focus on technical reason as itself inherently problematic, is circumspect and historical. At times he appears open to the idea that their analyses are persuasive representations of the negative impact of technology on modern society (e.g. Feenberg 2002: 19; 2010: 193; 2017: 69), writing that the 'basic claims' of Heidegger's apocalyptic opposition of technology to culture 'are all too believable' (1991: 7). His clearly stated position, however, is that these arguments mistakenly impute something perennial to technology that is actually contingent on its design under capitalism (Feenberg 2002: 21; 2010: 194–196),[3] and he repudiates the substantivist fallacy of 'opposing spiritual values to technology' (1991: 10). If such an opposition were integral there would be no possibility of technical politics, still less of the 'common ground between critical theory and the scientific and technical professions' (1991: 19) which, following Marcuse, Feenberg considers vital to it.

Feenberg's theory of the formal bias of technology is developed with these debates in the background. He seeks a theory that can account for the real and perceived implication of technology in the most problematic dimensions of modernity while at the same time holding open the possibility of new designs that will combine technical elements to solve human problems in ways that are not possible under capitalism. Feenberg wants to combine a sense of the gravity of humanity's current situation and of technology's implication in it, which is normally associated with cultural conservativism and political pessimism, with the optimism implicit in his thesis that rationalisation can be democratised.[4] In addition, the theory Feenberg elaborates has to have a degree of sociological precision when it comes to identifying how and why technology becomes problematic. This will free critical theory from its romantic, anti-technology past and enable it to acquire renewed political purchase, or as Feenberg puts it, critical theory will identify technology as, 'not a destiny but a scene of struggle' (Feenberg 1991: 14). Viewed in this way, the theory of formal bias is a main pillar of his project.

2 The theory of formal bias

Feenberg's rejection of essentialism must be distinguished from his discussion of substantivism and substantive bias. In philosophy of technology these two terms (essentialism and substantivism) are closely associated, because it would seem that if technology is always and everywhere in some sense pernicious, as essentialism claims, then this must correspond to substantive properties it possesses – that is to say, properties shared by all of its instances. Essentialists are committed to some kind of substantivism because they propound a non-relative property, or set of properties, as definitive of technology. However, substantivism need not entail essentialism. It is possible to maintain that technology always has some substantive impact and is therefore always ethically consequential (biased), without asserting that the character of this bias is always negative or regrettable.[5]

Feenberg associates substantivism with a kind of bias that might be found in social institutions or arrangements but which cannot exist in modern technological form. The pre-modern institutions referred to above might single out women or members of particular castes, for example, as unfit to own property or to have rights that other designated groups enjoy. Such social systems are designed by a biased intent. In *Between Reason and Experience* (2010), Feenberg argues that substantively biased reasoning like this simply could not enter the scene of technology design because were it to do so it would cause breakdowns and a loss of coherence in the resulting technology. He explains that 'substantively biased decisions in the technological realm, where cool rationality ought to prevail, lead to avoidable inefficiencies' (2010: 69).

Irrational hostility towards certain groups is grounded in feelings that would contaminate the kind of pure reflection on laws of motion of matter that is required to formulate a coherent technical design (2010: 163). Technical reason is irreducibly different from reasoning that includes a layer of feeling or prejudice. When Feenberg argues that technology is biased by contingent social factors specific to capitalism, he is not talking about prejudices or ideologies that issue from a ruling-class perspective on the world. Rather, the fact that technology requires a purely technical perspective leaves it peculiarly vulnerable to shaping by prevailing systems of thought and practice that are also unencumbered by values or meanings.

In place of substantive bias emanating from either irrational intentions at the scene of design or the purported negative essence of technology, Feenberg argues that modern technology is only ever formally biased. Formal bias 'prevails wherever the structure or context of rationalised systems or institutions favors a particular social group' (2010: 163). In other words, it occurs when a seemingly neutral system of rules is placed in a social context where it contributes to the systematic reproduction of unequal or unfair outcomes.

One possible point of confusion here concerns the role of the intentions that shape the technology. The point about intentions that produce formally biased design is that they are detached from their outcomes in the manner characteristic of modern, rationalised institutions. Technologists and others empowered to feed ideas into technology design do not often seek specific *social* benefits or prejudicial outcomes. Instead, their intentions are narrowly focused on efficiency gains that will result from the new technology. As empowered agents in a capitalist economy, they understand the potential in new techniques in terms of productivity and performance, which they dispassionately associate with enhanced control for management at the point of production (Feenberg 2010: 70). The association of the goal of enhanced control over a process or practice with management interests is mediated by scientific and technical discourses on management and workplace design. Feenberg argues that there is a kind of innate convergence of such discourses with the similarly value- and meaning-free orientation of technical reason itself (2010: 185).[6] These are the factors that shape technology design in modern capitalist economies, and the result is technology that enhances the operational autonomy of specific, privileged social groups (2010: 71).

Formally biased design is present where design shaped by this 'neutral' intention takes on a specific social function, namely that of unfairly enhancing what Feenberg calls the 'operational autonomy' (Feenberg 2002: 75–76)[7] of privileged groups in the production process. Feenberg emphasises the systematic, sociological character of formal bias, arguing that 'to show discrimination in the case of a technological choice ... it is necessary to demonstrate that the discriminatory outcome is no accident but reproduces a relationship of domination' (1991: 181). It occurs when a system designed to maximise efficiency, placed in a social context, serves to generate, amplify or reinforce patterns of inequality and unfairness. Formal bias is only present in technology design when both aspects of this definition are found together. Technology is biased even though (in fact, because) the intentions that shape it are neutral and, despite being mere physical matter configured in a certain way,[8] it operates to reproduce unfairness in a given social context (Feenberg 2002: 81–82).

Feenberg argues that formal bias has two forms, which he calls constitutive and implementation bias (Feenberg 2010: 164). In each case there is the determining intention just described and a social function defined in terms of the reproduction of social power relations. Constitutive formal bias occurs when 'values [are] embodied in the nature or design of a theoretical system or artifact' (Feenberg 2010: 163). Here the relevant test concerns whether it is conceivable that an artefact, placed in some other social context, might perform its function without systematically favouring the interest of a particular group over others. One of Feenberg's examples of such a system is the design of a production line which deskills workers and makes their lives unpleasant, while enhancing the operational autonomy of managers. Such a technology is constitutively biased because it is impossible to envisage a social situation where it might be used without having this effect. It is not substantively biased because it was not anyone's intention to design a system that would be unfair, or, rather, the design of the system was not motivated by a feeling or sentiment of hatred towards or fear of workers. What distinguishes substantively biased technology from constitutively formally biased technology is the presence or absence of such an intention (Feenberg 2010: 163). In this case, the motivation for the design is the 'neutral' one of making production processes more efficient.

It is not clear, however, that constitutive bias really is distinct from some kind of substantive bias. As discussed in the previous chapter, Marx (1990: 562) wrote of technology designed by capitalists with the aim of disempowering workers, breaking up their associations and reducing their capacity to subvert employer domination. The prime motivating element there seems to be fear, though the practical implications include increased profits and a measure of efficiency, narrowly construed. This combination of motives and affects in an intention would efface the distinction from substantive bias that Feenberg seeks to maintain. What has changed since Marx's time, perhaps, is that this mix of motivations and beliefs about economic practices and the merits of machinery is now routinely parsed through social science disciplines, especially management science and business studies. Feenberg treats the latter as discourses in the Foucauldian sense, as sites of condensation of knowledge and power.

Implementation bias differs from constitutive formal bias in that alternative implementations of the same artefact or design are conceivable without the unfair outcomes. Here, Feenberg writes that 'values [are] realized through contextualizations' (2010: 165). In other words, it is only when it is placed in a *specific* social context that the technology takes on its formally biased character. This is the kind of unfairness that results from designing a system that works well in one, imaginary setting but generates unanticipated negative consequences when ported to another. In my view, implementation bias is a clearer specification of what Feenberg originally intended by formal bias. In his first formulation of the theory he wrote that '[t]he essence of formal bias is the prejudicial choice of the *time, place and manner of the introduction of a relatively neutral system*' (1991: 180; emphasis in original text). In contrast, constitutive formal bias is inscribed in the design of a system and travels with it across contexts, indicating that it is actually somewhat ambiguous in relation to the rejected category of substantive bias.

Feenberg clarifies the difference between substantive and formal bias with reference to the intention embodied in a design. What makes technical systems formally biased is the absence of human values in them, rather than the impress of malicious or prejudicial purposes. Formal bias occurs despite the absence of such intentions. Sociologically, it is what happens when the capitalist motivation to secure profits through improved efficiency and enhanced control over production processes converges with the purported emptiness, or freedom from prejudice,

of technical reason. As seen above, Feenberg suggests that this conflu-
ence is a key dimension of societal rationalisation in the Weberian sense.
At the same time, however, his test for the presence of formal bias is a
thought experiment that involves asking of any given technical system
whether it might feasibly generate different outcomes under varied social
and cultural conditions, which would demonstrate that it is the location
of the system in a specific context that accounts for its role in producing
prejudicial social consequences (Feenberg 2002: 81).

The outcomes Feenberg is most concerned with here relate to the
enhanced operational autonomy of managers. Technology is biased in
context when we can see that the interests of a particular group are systematically favoured over those of others involved with the technology.
Most commonly, this involves managers gaining more control over production processes as a consequence of the application of scientific management and organisation principles. The latter are generic formulations
that enhance efficiency, in a narrow sense, in proportion as they abstract
the manager from production processes where they might have and feel
obligations to the people they work with. In this way, formal bias mirrors
societal rationalisation. As Feenberg puts it, 'formal bias prevails wherever the structure or context of rationalized systems or institutions favors
a particular social group' (2010: 163).

3 Operational heteronomy

There are, then, two aspects to formal bias, and both are necessary, while
neither is sufficient on its own, to produce it. First, there is the distinctive
kind of intention that shapes a technology design, namely one that is free
of concern with values and meanings and therefore dovetails with the
kind of thinking that needs to happen if there is to be technical design as
such. Second, formal bias only arises when, once set to work in a social
context, the resulting artefacts systematically enlarge the operational
autonomy of a social group.

The critical theory of technology is a normative theory, and its critical focus is on the biased nature of technology in capitalist society. It
is worth emphasising, therefore, that one of the – perhaps surprising –
consequences of the theory of formal bias is that it narrows the range
of cases with which the critical theory of technology is concerned. Even
technology designed with explicit nasty intent, for example, will be
deemed irrelevant if it does not have the requisite social consequences.
Technology with negative social consequences that are not the effect of
design informed by the valueless evaluations characteristic of modernity
will not feature in technical politics. Perhaps most importantly, technology that impacts negatively on specific groups in ways that are not

also advantageous to others by enhancing their operational autonomy will not be within the range of the theory.

It is also significant that the theory allows for a potentially quite large number of technologies that do not raise any normative issues. In principle at least, by insisting on the presence of a particular kind of intention in design and a specific kind of social outcome, Feenberg allows technology that might be considered 'neutral'. This seems to be unintentional, given his insistence that technology is socially shaped all the way down and his fundamentally agonistic conception of the social (considered further in the next chapter). Such technology might be comfortably accommodated in a pragmatic, Habermasian framework, within the normal development of a 'systems' sphere.[9]

Moreover, Feenberg rejects the possibility of designs that are motivated by or involve prejudicial intent, and insists that only what he calls 'cool rationality' (2010: 69) rules at the scene of design. I have indicated above that Marx's account of capitalist industrial machinery as designed to oppress workers would seem to be in tension with this requirement. Another example would be the printing technology described by Cynthia Cockburn (1983), which was designed with the malicious purpose of keeping women out of employment in nineteenth-century print factories. There, some machinery was kept deliberately and unnecessarily heavy as a result of agreements reached between unions and management. Since women were prohibited from working with machinery over a certain weight, better-paid work was thereby effectively reserved for male workers. In Feenberg's terms, the effect was to enlarge the operational autonomy of male workers, as well as managers and owners. In these examples, shaping intentions other than the one of cold neutrality appear to contribute to the regressive social outcome.

Feenberg addresses such cases through his category of constitutive formal bias, in which some groups of people are disadvantaged and excluded because designers fail to think about the variety of human beings who may be affected by or reliant upon the technology. In these cases bias is the result of neglect rather than malign intent, and Feenberg maintains that this kind of bias is most common in modern capitalism because of the focus on efficiency that dominates most thinking about technology and the narrow framing of the latter concept promulgated in disciplines like organisation theory and management science. He introduces the example of pavements that are too narrow to accommodate wheelchairs to elaborate on this (2010: 164). Another example might be the case of the Windows operating system, which disadvantaged blind and visually impaired computer users, putting many of them out of work (Goggin and Newell 2003).

Feenberg cites as an example of constitutive formal bias that is designed into the technology a case that is neatly analogous to Cockburn's example – that of factory machines designed to be used by children (2010: 163). The factory machines could be used by small adults or even, uncomfortably, by adults of average height, so that in principle they are only biased in context. The real biasing factor is not the shaping of the technology but its role in a context that includes a web of restrictive rules and conventions. In Cockburn's study she points out that male workers and trades unions sought to preserve their wages, rather than to exclude women, which tends to support such an interpretation.

Interestingly, however, in these cases, while the requirement of a neutral shaping intention is conserved, the clearest social consequence of the technology is not to enhance the power and privileges of a group but rather to adversely impact on a particular group, perhaps a minority. This would be better described as *operational heteronomy* than enhanced operational autonomy. It is quite conceivable, then, that technology could present no discernible benefit to ruling groups yet still have exclusionary or oppressive consequences for others.[10] In terms of Feenberg's theory, even when some technology negatively impacts certain groups more than others, perhaps obliging them to perform actions or tasks that others do not have to perform, it remains formally unbiased.

Feenberg's rejection of the category of substantive bias is, as was seen above, partly a result of his denial of any role for biased intentions in design, but it also follows from his insistence that bias is a contextual and not an essential property of technology. However, there are technology designs that are substantively biased in terms of his definition of the phrase and, in my opinion, they are too important for critical theory to overlook. An example of substantively biased technology in this specific sense is the mosquito device, which has been used in the UK to disperse groups of young people who are perceived as a nuisance by property owners.[11] The device emits a sound at a pitch that can only be heard by people under the age of 18. Changes in the human ear after that age mean that it becomes inaudible. The sound is, apparently, uncomfortable to those who can hear it and the device discourages young people from standing outside shops or on street corners where the owners do not desire their presence.

This technology was shaped by an intention that was at least in part motivated by negative feelings about a target group in the population. It worked with knowledge of something specific to them and identified that thing as a target. Even if this attitude was subordinate to the one of seeking a kind of control over social spaces, which might be cast as neutral, the intention to create a device that could only ever be experienced as uncomfortable by a specific group is surely prejudiced. The mosquito could be seen as enhancing the control of some groups of people, namely middle-class property owners, but a more exact description would be that it *limits and reduces* the autonomy of the targeted group. Moreover, the mosquito is substantively biased in the sense that variations in context do not change the fact that it only has adverse effects on a selected group in society and is therefore inherently prejudicial. While it is debatable whether it actually empowers anyone except in the most tendentious sense (the shopkeeper has the power to remove some people from the environment around his or her premises, but appreciating this as a 'benefit' seems to involve participating in paranoid and prejudiced fantasies), it is certain that it impacts negatively on the freedom of a targeted group to exercise the basic human right of association in a given public space.

Other examples of substantively biased technologies come from military designs. For example, the flechette is a particularly unpleasant kind of tank shell that is designed to disperse 4cm metal darts, which enter and can remain in targeted bodies. Once there, the shards of metal may take days or longer to kill. Although the rationale for the design of the flechette is that it enables offensive action against enemies concealed in dense foliage, it is difficult to see how the weapon constitutes any kind of an advance on regular shells, which can be so powerful as to assure complete destruction of their targets without taking the additional step of torturing them as well. The flechette would seem to be a clear case of substantive bias in technology design. It is inherently inhuman in its conception and design and so seems to be biased 'all the way down'; its cruelty is not something that it acquires only when placed in context.

It would be anomalous if the critical theory of technology pushed these and similar cases beyond the scope of its concerns. They are problematic for the theory because the intentions in their design are not neutral in the sense required for formal bias and because their social effects are unfair even though they do not obviously enhance anyone's operational autonomy in the sense Feenberg gives to that phrase.

What this discussion highlights is a discrepancy between the philosophical cast of Feenberg's theory and its reliance on sociological factors. The distinctions between varieties of formal bias and the rejected notion of substantive bias begin to break down on contact with the kinds of cases studied by social historians. Cockburn's study of print technology designed to exclude women highlights an aspect of design that seemingly eludes the theory of formal bias because of the theory's exclusive focus on enhancements to operational autonomy. The mosquito demonstrates the possibility of a technology that is biased by a malign intent and socially regressive without enhancing anyone's operational autonomy. Feenberg's reluctance to treat such negative and exclusionary impacts in themselves, independent of the question of how they are thematised in discourses of power, reflects the political orientation of his theory, especially its concern to identify potential sources of political agency.[12]

However, as presented, the theory of formal bias threatens to abstract technical politics from the sociological analysis of the dynamics of exclusion and disempowerment.

4 Dilemmas of containment

The examples of substantive bias just presented indicate the need to consider the possibility that technology will entail restrictions on the development of certain kinds of technology, perhaps similar to moves taken internationally to abolish land mines in the 1990s. One of the things that a critical theory of technology ought to be able to say is that designs like the mosquito and the flechette are not legitimate. Feenberg rejects containment mainly because he views it as a conservative strategy, alien to a critical theory that sides with progressive rationalisation. If these cases are important, however, then this is an important oversight. The politics of technology design must include space for such a proscriptive element.

Feenberg gives four reasons for rejecting containment as a strategy, and it is worth devoting some attention to them because of what they disclose about the broader orientation of his theory. First, he says that technical politics should not be conceived in terms that cast culture as resistant to technological innovations and change but should instead be concerned with a design politics whose goal is to identify and cultivate technology's currently neglected potentials. Here Feenberg aligns critical theory of technology with the Enlightenment belief in a positive directionality to the historical process based on the development of reason and deepening human understanding of the world. This casts critique and the advance of knowledge as breaking down 'traditional' barriers and overcoming 'substantively' instituted regimes of social power based on irrational prejudices and privileges. Such a view favours technology development rather than its inhibition and comports with Feenberg's positive focus on politicising technology design rather than simply opposing modern technology.

Second, Feenberg maintains that a containment stance perpetuates the opposition of cultural values to technology, while a progressive position envisages their reconciliation. For critical theory of technology, it should be conceivable that social values and goals would be entirely consistent with those of technology development, which is why it is important to break with essentialism. Third, he argues that it is impossible to specify at this or any point in history which domains of social and cultural life should be 'protected' from technology, since change is pervasive and what seems permanent and important today can turn out to have been transient and weightless tomorrow, and vice versa. Finally, containment presents the paradox of an instrumentally conceived preservation of the non-instrumental, which, Feenberg maintains, would have the perverse consequence of transforming the latter into a goal of technical action.

Feenberg rejects the idea of containment of technology by culture because he wants to distance the critical theory of technology from substantivist and conservative positions. However, he does acknowledge that there are occasions when containment of technology, in the form of an active proscription of some kinds of design, may be necessary. He writes that:

> Objects introduced to technical networks bear the mark of the functionalization to which they have been submitted. Not everything of value can survive that transformation. Hence, we reject the idea that more or less technically efficient means can best accomplish things such as forming friendships and enjoying Christmas dinner. (2010: 76)

This way of construing matters is, it seems to me, back to front. It is not necessary to invoke special domains of cultural practice to see the necessity of limiting or prohibiting certain technologies. Doing so plays into the hands of those critics who suggest Feenberg prevaricates over essentialism.[13] But the discussion in the previous section shows that inappropriate application of technical reasoning in human affairs is not the point at issue.

It is important to separate the idea that technology may be substantively biased from essentialist and conservative readings of that bias as located in technology's 'instrumental' character, which is held to contrast with other rationalities operative in special cultural domains, like the family or friendship relations. The point is not that such domains should be protected from technology in principle but rather that some technology is bad in itself and should be proscribed for that reason. Feenberg should be able to claim there are technology designs that are in conflict with the goals or rules of technology design, properly understood, in principle.

As Feenberg points out, technology only becomes threatening when its design reflects a particular disposition or cuts a certain kind of path through social relations. The way that it does this, when it becomes problematic, is specific to technology (other kinds of natural object and human artefact do not pose the same menace), but it is not caused by the technical reasoning involved in any technological project. It is not because of the reasoning behind technology that it can be disposed in this way but because of the specific entwinement of social purposes with physical properties in what Latour (2005) calls 'hybrid' combinations, which give rise to a distinctive kind of agency.[14] The mosquito illustrates that it can also involve a distinctive kind of social outcome, which is discriminatory in a negative sense, rather than primarily serving a positive interest.

This kind of bias extends beyond formal bias as Feenberg has presented the idea, since it involves recognising that, as post-phenomenological philosopher of technology Peter-Paul Verbeek points out (2006), technical objects *act* in ways that help some people and disadvantage others. They nearly always do this, and as such are inherently or substantively biased. At the same time, this is not substantive bias in the traditional sense: the cases discussed in this chapter reveal nothing about the 'essence of technology', except in the sense that they pertain to a particular modality of the intrusion of physical nature or brute causality into human affairs. Such intrusion can be associated with regret, especially when technology becomes a systematic agent of operational heteronomy. But equally, even 'good' technology would not be useful if it did not make a substantive difference with social consequences.

Verbeek argues that the complex imbrication of human intention and the agency of objects at the scene of design necessitates an ethical approach immanent to technology design practice. He presents his view as radically at odds with Feenberg's,[15] but detaching the definition of formal bias in terms of intentions and outcomes from the wider question of societal rationality makes it usable as the basis for just such an immanent ethical foundation. Feenberg's approach illuminates the range of intentions that might be present and suggests ways in which they might serve as conduits for unacknowledged social interests. Opening up the way in which an apparently narrow focus on 'technical objectives' might introduce foreseeable design bias is critical theory's distinctive contribution. It is not necessary to relate technical reasoning to wider historical developments to achieve this. Moreover, if it were true that prejudice could play no part in technology design because it is grounded in irrational feelings, this would also be problematic for Feenberg's project of a democratic transformation of technology, which surely presupposes a different mix of emotional, social and rational elements at the scene of design.

5 Immanent ethics of design

The emphasis, in the theory of formal bias, on a shaping intention makes it possible to articulate a formal principle that might realistically be operative within, or immanent to, the design process itself. Such an ethical principle might consist in something akin to the founding principle of Habermas's discourse ethics, according to which 'only those norms can claim to be valid that meet (or could meet) with the approval of all affected in their capacity as participants in a practical discourse' (Habermas 1990: 93). To suggest that something like this might be operative in technical design contexts is not to commit the 'fallacy of false concreteness',[16] but rather to claim that there are quasi-transcendental features of the technology design situation that ought to constrain what may reasonably be proposed there. Violation of this pragmatic foundation would involve the violator in a performative contradiction, in much the same way that some forms of political speech conflict with the rational foundations of democratic politics.

Just as Habermas (1990) distinguishes the rules of his ideal speech situation from the substantive principles discussed by participants in moral discourse, so Feenberg's theory of bias puts him in a position to advance similar rules as immanent to technical practice. There is a benign, transformative orientation towards the future that underscores all technical thinking and activity, which Feenberg draws out most effectively when he discusses medicine (2010: 81), writing that 'the value of healing practices presides over biological knowledge of the human body in medicine' (2010: 81). As such, technical activity contains implicit norms that can only be violated at the price of contradiction with the technological purpose itself, however this is manifest in a given society. This focus on immanent ethical foundations aligns Feenberg's theory with Habermas's pragmatic notion of 'quasi-transcendental' principles.

As we have seen, Feenberg includes a social dimension to the philosophical definition of technology, bringing it into dialogue with other disciplines, especially sociology. As David Stump points out, Feenberg's inclusion of a social dimension in the philosophy of technology is the single, 'most powerful and innovative aspect of his philosophy' (in Veak 2006: 5). To capitalise fully on it, however, he needs to go further in enriching his philosophy with sociology. Instead of deepening his engagement in this way, Feenberg chooses to embed the theory of bias in a historical conflict of rationalities. Drawing on Weber, he argues that modernity is defined by a capacity for conceptual distancing (2010: 173) that distinguishes modern societies from traditional ones, where the rationality involved in technical projects has not been 'purified' in 'technical disciplines' (2010: 177). Feenberg aligns this development to societal rationalisation, arguing that 'modern societies are unique in the exorbitant role they assign social rationality' (2010: 179).

However, a wealth of historical scholarship casts doubt on the distinction of modern from traditional societies in terms of the form of their technical knowledge. Martin Bernal (1987) famously demonstrated, for instance, that ancient cultures possessed advanced mathematics, which they used to make astronomical forecasts. Great engineering projects of the ancient world indicate high levels of technical understanding. Similarly, Zaheer Baber (1996) describes inoculation programmes in pre-colonial India, which presuppose medical knowledge, and Feenberg himself refers to proto-industrial activities in the pre-capitalist world, which could not have occurred without detailed knowledge of the production process. Numerous other examples can be produced of a kind of reasoning informed by abstract thinking in the centuries prior to modernity and in societies and cultures not normally included in it (e.g. Adas 1989; Baber 1996).

Feenberg emphasises (2010: 173) that he is not concerned to make a case for the cognitive superiority of modern societies; his focus is on the socio-cultural mediation of knowledge, and it is here that he considers they are distinctive in placing emphasis on the abstraction of function from meaning and codifying this into arcane disciplines that enforce social power. Detaching this argument from the notion of a wider societal rationalisation does not have to entail that modernity theory is abandoned altogether.[17] Marx's characterisation (Marx and Engels 1967) of modernity as a period of unprecedented rapid change, in which commodities become increasingly salient, is an alternative reading that does not invoke the rather obscure idea of society-wide transformations underpinned by a novel form of 'rationality' but instead concentrates on class antagonisms and social contradictions as the drivers of technical change. Feenberg's critical focus on the convergence of (neutral) technical reason with broad historical developments tends itself to abstract from the deep entanglements of technology with practices of domination.[18]

At the same time, Feenberg's introjection of a specifically sociological dimension into the philosophical definition of technology makes it possible to advance the claims of critical theory in more detailed, situated kinds of enquiry. However, one of the hazards of incorporating a social dimension into the definition of technology is that society changes, forcing amendments to the theory. Feenberg's concern with the operational autonomy of managers is a case in point because the interface of management and workplace technology has significantly altered in the last three to four decades, associated with digitisation or informationalisation of technology and related new management practices. This is reflected in changes to the discourse on management and organisations, which, as seen above, was pivotal to Feenberg's grasp of the biasing of technology in design.

Critical analysis of management science texts was one of the foundations for Luc Boltanski and Eve Chiapello's pathbreaking study, *The New Spirit of Capitalism* (2005). Feenberg has been fairly dismissive of this work,[19] but the challenge it presents to the category of operational autonomy is real. Increasingly, self-management, including a large degree of worker or user autonomy, is a presupposition of technology design.[20] Workers are now obliged to actively internalise system imperatives, converting them into personal norms of conduct. Meanwhile, contemporary work itself has to be seductive, appealing and exciting, leading some to characterise it as resembling an adventure, while others even write of a pervasive 'gamification' of the labour process.[21] This restructuring of work is part of the way that capitalism recuperated itself after the challenge it faced to its hegemony in the late 1960s and early 1970s. It entails new, 'streamlined' workers who use their autonomy to benefit the system because they have internalised its values (competitiveness, esteem for material success, etc.), incorporating them into their sense of themselves in a way that represents a new level of penetration of societal demands into individual psychology and interpersonal relationships.[22] All this has implications for the theory of bias in technology design.

Feenberg's vision is partly inspired by these developments, in the sense that he prefers to think through the transformation of technology in terms of a widening of the cultural and normative inputs to the scene of design rather than advocating a defensive, conservative strategy aimed at limiting the development of new technologies. However, there is a tension between his declaration of the impossibility of substantive bias and his vision of a future technology shaped by wider values.

Democratising technology opens the way to designs (Feenberg sometimes calls them 'concretisations') that incorporate ethical and aesthetic values excluded from modern technology. This, he suggests, will create 'a new direction of technological progress' (2002: 150), which he calls 'progressive rationalisation'.

There is a kind of implicit, positive substantive bias in this vision of a society in which 'values would be installed in the technical disciplines themselves' (2010: 81). In the society of the future, technology that promotes equality, for example, will not be less subject to social distortion than contemporary technology. Rather, such technology would harness the agency of physical objects to benefit some, currently disadvantaged, social groups rather than others. Feenberg shies away from utopian speculation on these possibilities, preferring to identify interventions that challenge 'elite power structures inherited from the past in technically rational forms' (2010: 71). But what Boltanski and Chiapello's work demonstrates is that in many ways this technocratic form of social organisation is already largely superseded in informational capitalism, while the need for technical politics remains urgent.

In this chapter I have argued that in the theory of formal bias, Feenberg includes a sociological dimension in the philosophical definition of technology, while making a decisive move to free the critical-theoretic conception of technology from its essentialist, dystopian heritage. This opens up a perspective in which it is possible to clarify the combination of ruling intention and sociological outcome that characterises systematic and pervasive bias in technology design. To some extent these achievements are concealed by Feenberg's attachment to the transcendental thesis of a historically ambivalent societal rationalisation. As technology sheds its association with bureaucracy and top-down management processes in the real world, however, it becomes possible to sharpen focus on an ethics immanent to technology design, an idea that is crucial to Feenberg's theory of technical politics.

Notes

1 Habermas writes that the task of philosophy today is to 'mediate intepretively between expert knowledge and an everyday practice in need of orientation' (1992: 17–18).
2 This is a very different line of attack to that of Marx, a difference Feenberg neglects to examine. As we saw in the previous chapter, Marx described a direct, intentional shaping of technology by capitalists, the substantive consequence of which was machines that were horrible to work with and limited workers' abilities to influence the production process or to build effective solidarity with one another.
3 It's important to note that this distinction is also present in Adorno, for whom technological rationality has a 'historical essence' (2000: 25). Defenders of Heidegger maintain that he also is not an essentialist, and Iain Thomson alleges that Feenberg 'simply us[es] essentialism as a descriptive term to characterize a fairly wide range of theories about technology with which he disagrees' (in Veak 2006: 65).
4 The sense of this claim will be explored in the next two chapters.
5 This conflicts with an intuitive sense that all bias is wrong because it involves systematic disadvantage to some individuals or groups, played out in ways that are not thematised and legitimated through public discourse. However, I would contend that all societies include bias in this sense in their fundamental structures and this is not always a matter of normative concern. A socialist society would institute measures to systematically prevent the materially better-off from gaining further advantage: indeed, if it failed to establish such bias it would not warrant the name 'socialist'. These arrangements would not be regrettable because they were not discussed on a regular basis.
6 It might seem as if technical reason is then an essential and indeed substantive property. Feenberg's proposal is that it is a *historical essence* in the sense discussed above – that is, it becomes an essential feature with the emergence of the modern social formation.
7 Feenberg takes this phrase from organisation theory (personal correspondence).
8 Latour argues that technology's behaviour in any situation is not susceptible, merely by dint of its material or substantive nature, to proper explanation by seemingly applicable scientific or causal laws. In his view, the reality in excess of science mournfully identified as essential yet unattainable by critical theorists is directly accessible now, in the sense that much of practical life already operates with a reality that ranges beyond what is sanctioned by the regime of epistemology, and always did (Latour 2013b: 70–71; 85). At one point he even observes that the 'material world' is simply not big enough to accommodate the multiple 'modes of existence' produced by actors (2013b: 103). Here as elsewhere, however, Latour neglects the practical entanglement of questions about the validity of knowledge with those concerning the operation of power.

9 Feenberg tends not to acknowledge this, perhaps because he has a polemical interest in charging other second- and third-generation critical theorists with neglecting technology. Once recognised, though, it becomes a matter of judgement how important the critique of technology is to the wider project of developing a critical theory of society. Notwithstanding this, detaching the critique of technology from global claims about the evils of societal rationalisation is a theoretical advance implicit in the theory of formal bias which, in my view, Feenberg does not fully capitalise on.

10 Such negative effects will remain out of view until they are successfully highlighted by the affected groups. Feenberg's neglect of this category turns out to be telling in an important respect, since it highlights the disjunct between the critical theory of technology as formulated and sociological analysis of the processes whereby injustice gets thematised by affected parties in the first place. Since the theory excludes technology that is not currently perceived as problematic, it seems to lack the resources to account for the struggle those subject to operational heteronomy face to articulate their concerns and gain recognition for them. I revisit this point in the next chapter, on technical politics.

11 The device has been banned in some European countries. See www.guardian. co.uk/society/2010/jun/20/teenager-repellent-mosquito-banned-europe. Accessed 19 June 2012.

12 This reproduces Marcuse's focus on the radical political potential of technical elites.

13 For example, David J. Stump writes that Feenberg 'keeps the general analytic framework that essentialism makes available while rejecting essentialism' (in Veak 2006: 8).

14 In other words, it is possible to say that there is something specifically technological about the way that some technologies are bad, without thereby claiming that there is badness in all technology.

15 In a review article Verbeek (2013) misrepresents Feenberg as the exponent of an unreconstructed modernism in which the sterile oppositions of traditional critical theory are all intact. I discuss the real differences between the two further in Chapter 5.

16 Habermas applies this phrase to arguments that purport to identify actual situations corresponding to his ideal speech situation.

17 As recommended by Latour (1993).

18 The identification of technology with the allegedly distinctive rationality of modernity is a bugbear of critical theory that limits its contemporary relevance – a point I return to in Chapter 4.

19 Curiously, Feenberg maintains (in Khatchatourov 2019) that studying management science literature, which is their principal methodology, is not a good way to understand contemporary labour processes and argues that the fundamental dynamics of workplace control have not shifted since the pioneering studies carried out in the 1950s and 1960s (Braverman 1974). It is worth noting that already in the 1960s Marcuse had observed that technology demanded that workers participate more in their own subjection as part of the modern industrial production process (Marcuse 1964: 30).

20 Boltanski and Chiapello overlook the issue of technology, neglecting to consider the ways in which the changes they describe to the labour process have been facilitated by new technology and have themselves shaped things like user interface design and the highly specific and limited use society has made of networked computing.
21 See Kirkpatrick (2015) for discussion of this and critical theory's response.
22 Sometimes grasped in terms of 'neo-liberal governmentality'; see e.g. Dardot and Laval (2014).

3

Technical politics

Technical politics is the central concept of Feenberg's critical theory of technology, the point around which everything else turns. Even the ontological dilemmas in his theory are resolved here, in his thinking of the technical *as* political. Whereas earlier critical theorists perceived technology as the most dense point in a system that smothered the human capacity for self-emancipation, Feenberg argues that it now presents openings for democratic intervention, and he puts forward a strategic, political conception of the kinds of dispute over technology design and use that are increasingly common in digital culture. Feenberg's project differs markedly from that of earlier critical theories, then, in finding overt political significance in technical practices.

To develop critical theory in this direction, Feenberg advances a distinctive concept of hegemony, a close conceptual relative of the idea of reification discussed in Chapter 1 (Section 2). As we saw in the last chapter, the bias of technology is maintained by a sheen of neutrality that ensures it comes to appear necessary while resistance to it seems nothing short of irrational. This reified appearance can be broken down in practice when people engage in active experiences that move beyond compliance and become experimental. In this way, technical activity has the potential to become a form of political praxis, breaking the hold of controlling illusions. Once people learn to dabble in technologies and to achieve more with their devices than the set of functions stipulated by the manual[1] then technological reality begins to come into focus. That reality is one of indeterminacy and open-ended experimentation, in which objects are remediated by their users and may become resistant to the identities imposed on them by manufacturers, corporations and governments.

Reconfiguration of their sensuous relationship with devices and machines dissolves the illusion of objective necessity and points technology users towards further experimentation and alternative possible uses. This dissolution of technology's authority in a popular culture of hacking and dabbling is, in Feenberg's theorisation, a political process. People breaking the rules of technology use has consequences which, taken in the round, constitute an extension of democracy. Feenberg argues that technology as currently designed is a key element in the main-tenance of political hegemony and that popular technical interventions are subversive of this. Progressive technical politics involves articulating and channelling these interventions into a concerted struggle against technological hegemony.

The concept of hegemony is central to Feenberg's thesis that popular interventions in technical domains constitute the principal form of authentic politics in contemporary societies. Hegemony, as formulated by Marxist theorist Antonio Gramsci, is a form of domination that works through cultural media of representation.[2] A party or social class is hegemonic when its favoured version of the elements of cultural life, in which a society represents itself to its members, are embraced and accepted by the majority. There is a clear affinity between this idea and formal bias, in which specific designs present themselves as the neutral form of current technical capabilities and this appearance of neutrality is a sheen on injustice and exclusion. Hegemony is a political concept, though, and understanding how it works gives insight into its thoroughly contested character and the possibility of political strategies based on this. Section 1 describes Gramsci's theory and provides a brief discussion of his understanding of the role of technology in maintaining capitalist domination.

Feenberg extends the idea of hegemony into the domain of modern technology design and use through his idea of the technical code, which is the focus of Section 2. The technical code structures the field of tech-nical politics. Its impress is what connects individual technologies into the wider web of connected artefacts that constitutes the technical in modern societies. It is written into all objects that are recognisable as tech-nology. As previously noted, as code it is both determinate for the social position of the artefact, conferring upon it a certain reified status in the eyes of its human users, *and* subject to modification by them – it can be rewritten. It is in grasping the space of underdetermined play with tech-nical elements, and the possibility of multiple alternative concatenations of elements into designs that may serve different purposes, that Feenberg finds the radical potential in constructivism.

As discussed in Chapter 1, constructivist studies of social shaping identify the social processes that constitute new technologies in devel-opment. Viewed through the lens of critical theory, constructivist studies display the reality of technology as a social process as against its conven-tional appearance as a realm of reified facts that embody and corroborate established ways of doing things. The idea of the technical code, which works through the agency of constructivism's social groups to 'condense' particular social values with technical considerations in specific designs, politicises constructivism's central insights.

Section 3 discusses the relationship between technical politics and Ernesto Laclau and Chantal Mouffe's (1985) theory of radical democracy. Their famously 'post-Marxist' interpretation of the politics of counter-hegemony is focused on the capacity of political discourse to produce radical re-articulations of dominant ideas aimed at shifting the dominant conception of society, which they construe as a limit or horizon, in order to change the prevailing sense of what is possible. Feenberg adapts these ideas to advance his idea of democratic technical politics as a series of contests for control over the technical code. This involves synthesising the idea of the technical code with the concept of political hegemony.

According to Feenberg, hegemony in contemporary societies is technological in character. The technical code is open to contestation and dispute, as constructivist analyses show, but these disputes go on under a horizon that limits what can count as a valid intervention or a legitimate technical statement. Just as political discourse has rules that constrain what may be said and done as consistent with social reality, so only some kinds of action will be recognised as technical. This sense of what technology is (its identity) is how human beings experience the weight of what Feenberg calls hegemonic technological rationality. It is the culturally dominant, hegemonic articulation of the technical code and, as such, it pervades people's experiences with modern technology.

On Laclau and Mouffe's understanding of the political, it involves changing the way that society is experienced as real – that is, the nature and position of the limit it sets on what may be proposed and what may be done. The politics of articulation involve attempts to shift this boundary by loosening the hold of hegemonic equivalences and creating spaces for excluded and suppressed experiences to gain expression. This resonates with Feenberg's search for a bridging concept between the small-scale disputes over individual artefacts described by constructivism and the wider concern with democratic change that defines his critical theory.

Section 4 examines Feenberg's synthesis of Laclau and Mouffe's concept of politics with the issue of technological transformation. The political theory of radical democracy rests on a distinctive ontology, which is the notion of a necessary yet intolerable absence, and this negative ontological premise is central to Feenberg's thought. Just as political institutions, law, morality and other 'superstructural' layers are social products perceived and lived as ontological givens over which people have no control, so technology is a reified social product. Just as radical democracy tries to shift the limits of what the state and other institutions can do, and even the form they can take, by creating subversive articulations of political discourse, so democratic technical politics is aimed at moving what Feenberg calls the 'boundary of technique' towards a more ambitious, more humane technology than the machines that have been produced to date.

Section 5 explores Feenberg's understanding of the goal of the technical politics of transition, which he sometimes characterises as 'civilisational change'. At this point in the theory he posits a kind of aggregate outcome for the various fronts of struggle and contestation opened up by democratic technical politics. Just as the technical code involves a series of equivalences and articulations that reproduce modernity's idea of itself as 'technological civilisation', so, Feenberg argues, socialist civilisation will manifest the unity of a different hegemonic ordering defined by a culture of vibrant democratic participation and a humanised aesthetic. In conclusion, the chapter lodges some reservations about the viability of technical politics, asking in particular if Feenberg moves too quickly to a political theorisation of technical practices at the cost of a neglect of social factors that bear upon exclusion and marginalisation in technical culture.

1 Hegemony and technology

The principal source for the concept of hegemony is Antonio Gramsci, a Marxist thinker of the 1920s and 1930s, contemporary with Lukàcs. Whereas the latter, and later the Frankfurt School, concerned themselves with the cultural ramifications of reification, Gramsci's main focus was on political strategy.[3] The key question that confronted all of these thinkers was how to move from multiple specific practices in which the dominant illusion, or the illusions that sustained domination, were decomposed and broken down to a broader perspective that applies the same realism to the question of the character of society as whole. Feenberg draws on the idea of hegemony to advance a strategic conception of technical politics, in which hacktivist and grass roots technical interventions and movements are connected through an internal logic that points towards wider change.

In practice, the experience of an individual or a group of workers includes demystification, in the sense that they really get to know how things work (or don't) and view management ideas, for example, with a healthy scepticism. Extending such demystification into a critical perspective on society at large is not straightforward because of reification and the hold of dominant ideological representations. As we have seen, the Frankfurt School largely neglected to explore this as a political question, considering such a level of thematisation as essentially out of reach in a society where every successful intervention was liable to be rapidly commodified and brought under control by the system. According to them, the irrational and all-encompassing character of the system could only be glimpsed through critical reflection, mediated by difficult art and theory, not opposed or countered directly through political practice.

Gramsci's theory of hegemony is a strategic rethinking of the political with the more orthodox Marxist aim of creating a political revolution out of social praxis. He describes hegemony as a condition in which 'the development and expansion of one particular group are conceived of, and presented, as being the motor force of a universal expansion, of a development of all the "national" energies' (1982: 182). Under modern conditions political power is secured by the social class that succeeds in working the weave of representations that comprise a national culture so as to create the impression that their interests are those of society as a whole. The autonomy of the political and its distinctive logic are located in the struggle to achieve this. For political representatives of the working class it involves using elements of popular culture to break down the appearance of necessity that attaches to social relations as currently constituted, in order to supplant it with a vibrant sense of the alternative social orderings that are possible.

Writing when Fordist production methods were revolutionising the modern factory, Gramsci already noticed the essential role of new technology in forging the hegemony of the capitalist class. Building on Marx's observation that the power of the workers comes to appear to them as an alien force owned by the bourgeoisie, Gramsci notes that industrial technology reinforces each individual worker's sense of their own contribution as minuscule and unimportant, while their appreciation of the productive capacity of the system is magnified so that it seems overwhelming, like an objective force of nature.[4] This appearance, he says, is an effect of social power combined with the awesome scale of the new mechanised form of production. In reality, new technology is a historical product and it can be broken down:

> For the individual worker, the junction between the requirements of technical development and the interests of the ruling class is 'objective'. But this junction, this unity between technical development and the interests of the ruling class is only a historical phase of industrial development, and must be conceived of as transitory. The nexus can be dissolved; technical requirements can be conceived in concrete terms, not merely separated from the interests of the ruling class, but in relation to the interests of the class which is still subaltern. (Gramsci 1982: 202)

In this way technology was already, in Gramsci's writings, one of the elements in a prevailing hegemony: a weaving together of specific societal interests into a distinctive formation in which one class achieves dominance by seeming to incarnate the objective interests and concerns of the whole.

The essential dynamic in the theory of political hegemony is the periodic dissolution of seemingly objective and immutable structures through a process of critical action that proceeds in the first instance by unlocking ideas and modes of thought in the political subject. Through revolutionary praxis (that is, action that anticipates or prefigures a superior way of life)[5] the greater realism and authenticity of that way of living is demonstrated and experienced in practice. Alternative representations of reality then become possible, even necessary, to make sense of this experience, and in Gramsci's theory this is political.

2 Politicised constructivism: the technical code

As Feenberg points out (1995), technocracy was the dystopian cultural backdrop that informed the thinking of the previous generation of critical theorists. As the physical incarnation of a pervasive instrumentalism that menaced meaning and threatened to leave society at the mercy of experts whose only concern was efficiency, technology appeared to be beyond reform. In this context, theorists' efforts were largely aimed at defending the possibility of non-technological meaning-making as the true human vocation.[6] For Feenberg, however, disputes over the meaning of any given technology promise to change the global meaning of technology itself and, ultimately, even hold out the possibility of a change of civilisational model.

In effect Feenberg inverts critical theory's attitude towards technology by identifying it as the locus of political opportunity for radical social and cultural transformation. This move is made possible in large part by his engagement with constructivism, especially the principle that for any problem a technological capability might be used to solve there will invariably be more than one equally feasible design. Social actors select from among the available alternatives, and in this way technology is shaped by, rather than determining of, social relations.

Constructivism places emphasis on how technologies are described by groups of people and on the social processes through which these descriptions become stabilised. Constructivist studies identify the emergence of more than one distinctive vocabulary applied to a technology in its development phase and show how different social groups prefer some descriptions to others because those descriptions tend to produce artefacts that comport with the interest they take in the technology. Once a particular description takes hold, artefacts are reshaped to better suit the interests of the winning group, and in this way their shaping is both symbolic and material.[7] A new technology is said to be 'stabilised' when one way of describing it becomes dominant, fixing its identity.

For Feenberg, the importance of constructivism lies in the way that these studies break down the illusion of necessity that inheres in technologies once the shaping process has achieved closure in this way. The authority of technology is undermined by awareness of its contingency on social choices made by human beings, and this is a crucial step in countering its reification – the appearance that technology is something people have to submit to and work with, rather than a thing they might be involved in shaping. The pre-eminence of language in these explanations adds to the feeling of arbitrariness in the events they describe; in effect, social actors might make any kind of sense they like when confronted with a new artefact.

Constructivism has been criticised for detaching its fables of invention and technology development too radically from any wider social picture (Winner 1993). The appeal of constructivist narratives lies at least partly in the way that social groups are manifest in descriptions and appear themselves as social constructs that emerge in the course of engagement with the nascent artefacts. Cycling communities, for example, form around the emergent bicycle rather than as combinations of human individuals already laden with pre-established social histories that affect their attitudes and behaviours. Partly to remedy this, Feenberg folds the basic insights of constructivism into a richer theorisation by replacing the openness of natural language with the Foucauldian notion of discourse and with his own idea of the 'technical code'.

The technical code is centrally concerned with how values get impressed on artefacts at the scene of design and the related question of how technology as a whole comes to be aligned with dominant social groups and to serve their interests. Feenberg agrees with constructivism that technology is shaped by social processes all the way down: there is no, 'inviolate level' (Feenberg 2010: xxiii) of purely technical determination that ensures any one design will be selected from the range of equally effective options.[8] For Feenberg, constructivism's focus on 'socially relevant groups' abstracts our understanding of social shaping from wider social networks and webs of meaning. Indeed, such is their excessive focus on the sociological minutiae of each case that some constructivist studies even lose sight of anything that connects the disparate instances of technology as technology.[9]

In contrast, Feenberg maintains that the technical code is manifest wherever social interests are at work shaping technology designs. Feenberg describes it as 'the realization of an interest in a technically coherent solution to a general type of problem' (Feenberg 2002: 15). On one side, then, the technical code constitutes some objects as technical, which obliges a certain kind of response from human agents. On the other side, the object's status as technical is conditional on agents responding in this way by incorporating it into their technical practices.

Resulting designs bear the impress of the technical code and, as a result, they are in alignment with and re-enforce the current social and political hegemony.[10] As well as informing the actions of proximal social actors, each manifestation of the code 'serves as a paradigm or exemplar for a whole domain of technical activity' (Feenberg 2002: 20).

The 'code' metaphor includes three related sets of ideas. First, as discussed in the previous chapter, 'it is most essentially the rule under which technical choices are made in view of preserving operational autonomy' (Feenberg 1991: 80). Here the emphasis is on the routinisation of design practice so that choices result in artefacts that support and re-enforce existing power structures. Second, while artefacts are shaped to facilitate the pursuit of certain ends, they must also communicate their function to other social actors and enrol them in relevant activities.[11] Feenberg writes that 'organisations must encode their technical environment, not merely associating technology with certain signifiers, but installing these signifiers in its very structure' (1991: 81). Finally, the technical code is a discourse in the Foucauldian sense; it is 'a "regime of truth" which brings the construction and interpretation of technical systems into conformity with the requirements of a system of domination' (1991: 79). Here the technical code extends beyond local sites of technology design and is inscribed in norms of perception and practice that pertain to technology but are operative over wide social domains.[12]

Feenberg writes that 'Modern societies ... build long networks through tightly coupling links over huge distances between very different types of thing and people' (2010: 76). The technical code runs through these networks, controlling the description and shaping of new artefacts, where it is a rule of participation: the appearance of technology *qua* technology, where it is a kind of signification, and extending to the sociocultural horizon, where it places technology in the categorial ordering specific to that society's idea of itself, or its imaginary. At each of these points the technical code is met by countervailing forces that may affect its operation.

For example, a society might become 'more technological', altering the place of technology on its horizon. Feenberg argues that modern societies think of themselves in this way, and that this difference from other cultures (classed as 'traditional') then becomes a matter of identity for people. Similarly, people's expectations and perceptions of what counts as a technology may be altered as a result of ideological or political pressure. Feenberg gives the example of environmentalism, which he says has succeeded in installing the question of sustainability close to the heart of what technology means. Constructivists have shown that disputes arise all the time when new artefacts are in development. Feenberg's theory shows that these conflicts stand in a wider context, and that the technical code 'invisibly sediment[s] values and interests in rules and procedures, designs and artefacts that routinize the pursuit of power and advantage by a dominant hegemony' (1991: 14).

While the outcomes of the contests described by constructivism are not determined, struggles over the meaning of technologies are waged in a distinctive social context. The fact that they are technical in character constrains the choices made by those involved in the design process, ensuring that some values (and corresponding social interests) are more likely to prevail than others. The scene for constructivist struggles has been set, so to speak, by the previous history of such struggles, since these leave a legacy that is both technical and social in character. The technical code, therefore, is always already hegemonic. As Feenberg puts it, 'Since technology is not neutral but fundamentally biased towards a particular hegemony, all action undertaken within its framework tends to reproduce that hegemony' (Feenberg 2002: 63). The prevailing logic of technology design, which he calls hegemonic technological rationality, ensures that the values of managerial control, a narrowly defined idea of efficiency, and a stern absence of other values are pervasive at the scene of design.

However, the fact that a hegemonic order exists and is inherited from the past does not mean that it cannot be challenged. An important point of introducing the code metaphor is precisely this. Using the idea that technology is a constitutive codification of certain objects enables Feenberg to characterise struggles over design as a particular kind of contest with distinctive rules. Regardless of whether social actors realise it or not, in the many small disputes that mark technology design and use, the meaning of technology is at stake and open to change.

3 Technical democracy

The idea of the technical code is therefore pivotal for Feenberg's thesis that disagreements over nascent technology design are not mere historical curiosities but, potentially at least, matters of political importance. He develops this insight into a theory of technical politics by drawing on Ernesto Laclau and Chantal Mouffe's development of the idea of hegemony. For them, 'the concept of hegemony supposes a theoretical field dominated by the category of *articulation*' (Laclau and Mouffe 1985: 93). Their emphasis on articulation grasps the autonomy of political action from infrastructural determinants, while the move to autonomise what might once have been called the ideological 'superstructure' defines their post-Marxism.

Focusing on language as the medium of politics,[13] Laclau and Mouffe argue that emancipatory struggle has moved from being a matter of rival, class-based articulations of the elements of political discourse, as Laclau had suggested in earlier work (1979), to being one in which articulation of difference is the measure of radicalism. According to this theory, the discursive coherence of politics is obtained at the price of fixity, which might be thought of as upholding the law of identity in the field of political and cultural representation. It necessarily entails the withholding of recognition to marginal or misrepresented groups, or to the validity of their claims of unfair treatment. Hegemony is established when antagonism over who and what gets to 'appear' in politics, and get counted as important enough to matter,[14] is placed out of view by the operation of power. The idea of society as a given, beyond the reach of contingency and articulation, then emerges as a kind of horizon on legitimate political activity.

In this understanding, radical democracy is a permanent political struggle to reopen the question of who and what counts and gets included in politics. Radical democracy succeeds in its struggle against hegemony when 'social logics replace ontological foundations' (Laclau and Mouffe 1985: 183). Prevailing conceptions of what counts as possible or realistic can be changed, and the hold of a narrow, 'common sense' view of society upheld by politics can be loosened by a political practice that deploys strategic re-articulations of the elements of political discourse. When what matters in politics is extended to include new groups and non-traditional concerns, there is a corresponding alteration to the meaning of 'society' and to the kind of limit this represents. The theory of hegemony maintains the neutrality of the elements of political discourse until they are combined in determinate articulations, which can reflect either this focus on difference or the attempt to close it down and affirm established identities.

This conception of politics as an agonistic, discursive practice shaped by articulation mirrors Feenberg's notion of formal bias in technology design. As seen in the last chapter, he emphasises that the technical code works through concatenations of neutral technical components, which produce designs that are only biased in context. Interestingly, however, Laclau and Mouffe exclude technology from the field of contingency and articulation. The struggle for hegemony is waged in terms of control over syntactical elements of political discourse, and while the areas of life that are open to articulation in that way expands in the capitalist era,[15] it does not extend to those dimensions of the social formation that are paradigmatic, or systematised. For this reason, they exclude things like the 'reorganization of an ensemble of bureaucratic administrative functions according to criteria of efficiency or rationality' (1985: 136) from the politics of hegemony because such practices are not located in contingency.[16]

Undeterred, Feenberg presents the struggle over the meaning of technology as an instance of hegemony and radical democratic counter-articulation. Hegemony is a form of power that operates through media (popular culture, political 'news' media or indeed technology) in which opposed parties find themselves operating. The idea of hegemony enables a rethinking of power in terms of strategic dynamics rather than as a matter of static, structural confrontations of parties with clear and opposed interests deriving from an exploitative economic base. It rests on a conception of politics as autonomous from economic and social correlates, and as a domain that involves participants making plays for a kind of positive association, or equivalence, with key elements of the surrounding culture. By appearing to be more in tune with the concerns of the people as a whole, a party or group can shift the ground of debate and ultimately win control of the state. In this way, political parties present themselves as sharing meanings with the populace. For radical democrats, winning hegemony involves such a play of ideas to win recognition for groups that have been excluded from political representation. Success in this will change the meaning of 'society' and at the same time shift the prevailing idea of what is possible. Laclau and Mouffe argue that this strategic conception of politics is superior to a more Marxist approach that makes direct, reductive appeal to class or other interests.

Just as with the terms of political discourse, hegemony in technology design works through the imposition of a determinate articulation of elements that reflect the interests of one group, while excluding those who do not count.

The technical code defines the meaning of technology and sets limits on what it can be expected to do, in the same way that political hegemony encourages a restricted idea of what society can be. As Gramsci already understood, the illusion that technology is an independent power over which people can exercise no control plays a key role in both these scenarios. The phases of a standard constructivist account of technology development can be recast in light of Laclau and Mouffe's ontology of lack, disclosing their fuller, theoretical significance.

For them, political struggle emanates from a primal antagonism that is held out of view by politics. This antagonism is, in their terms, displaced by political agonistics.[17] The goal of radical democracy is to change the terms of this displacement, so that those who have traditionally only been subject to domination by hegemonic power can instead play an active role in shaping society. The notion of a realm of antagonism that is located outside the field of representation but which nonetheless shapes it applies equally well to technology. Faced with absence, or a generalised incapacity in the face of nature, there is perhaps an omnipresent struggle to create, to make something out of nothing, which is primal to the human condition yet poorly understood.

Enigmatic and in some ways unrepresentable, invention gives rise to new technological elements which form the basis of the competitive dispute between 'relevant social actors' described by constructivism. In the early stages of a technology, often the focus of constructivist studies, design appears to be an open field associated with free creativity and play unencumbered by substantive or historical determinants. This is covered over when the process becomes agonistic, or in constructivist terms when the meaning of an invention is questioned and disputes arise, perhaps fuelled by a justified sense that different, equally practicable designs working with the same capabilities serve opposed social interests.

Establishing the dominant, hegemonic image of technology as a whole (in modern societies as the authoritative and exclusive domain of expertise) is both a condition of victory in this struggle and one of its outcomes. When technology has been subject to hegemonic codification this is because creativity and experimentation have given way to conflict over meaning and representation, culminating in the decisive impress of hegemony. This is understood by constructivism as 'stabilisation'. At this point, the technical code confers a seemingly fixed, ontologically certain identity on the resulting technology, making it appear as part of the technological given and, as such, immutable and beyond question.

Feenberg envisages progressive technical politics as attracting 'a democratically constituted alliance of actors, embracing all those affected' (2010: 80) by specific technologies. Technical politics is a matter of introducing different social logics into the operation of the technical code and, in this way, changing what counts as legitimate technical practice. He gives a number of examples of this, such as his account of Minitel users who transformed an early French computer network from an electronic phone book into a dating agency (Feenberg 1995, chapter 6). In so doing, he argues, they shook the equipment free from its symbolic association with the state, organisation and efficient communication and broadened its range of uses. He also discusses the example of HIV and AIDS patients (1995: chapter 5) who, faced with the prospect of having to wait for new drugs to pass through extensive trials, campaigned to change the rules on drug testing so that they could participate and, in so doing, gain earlier access to life-saving medicines.

In both these cases technical practices were opened up and modified by groups who had previously been thought of merely as recipients of technologies. Their activities were aimed at securing a more active role in which they gained representation as agents who could 'speak' for themselves, and as a result they reconfigured the operation of the technical code. The first changed the image of the computer network, overwriting predefined functions and forcing it to accommodate communicative cultural uses. The second asserted an active role for patients in choosing what level of risk they were prepared to take in their search for a cure. In both cases this re-articulation of the code creates equivalences (networks = communication = culture; experiment = risk = choice) that were not salient in the previous order of things. It is by no means implausible, if a little bit speculative, to suggest that these local changes were associated with wider changes to the meaning of technology, reflected in the place people subsequently assigned to it in their mental image of society.

Feenberg suggests that examples like this illustrate the possibility of a democratic challenge to the operation of the technical code. He gives several reasons for construing matters in these terms. First, the presence of more people in the design process will in itself have consequences for the technical code because larger groups will be more sensitive to risks presented by new technologies. More vulnerable members of society are often disproportionately affected by such hazards, so their inclusion in the design process will mitigate this. In this way, wider public involvement will necessarily create resistance internal to the design process. The overall goal of radical democratic technical politics is to safeguard the scene of design so that it is free from influence by powerful social groups. Success in this should be seen as creating a 'protective umbrella under which social creativity can operate at the micro-level of particular institutions and workplaces' (Feenberg 1991: 61).

Potential is protected beneath the umbrella and glimpsed in different articulations of the technical code. Resistance to dangerous or hazardous innovations, for example, might tip over into different articulations, as when workers succeed in imposing safety standards on the design of boilers. New potentials that would be overlooked by the existing hegemony become available in the course of the design process and might, in principle, be developed at any time. Feenberg is cautious on this point, however, because the aggregate effect of multiple new articulations expressing counter-hegemonic social logics that will 'guide the design of future technology' (1991: 125) would be a new technical code, producing different rules for the selection and concatenation of technical elements. It is more important to retain the idea of potential as something that haunts the current hegemony than to linger too long on the question of its possible future as a new, utopian technology – a point I return to in Chapter 5.

The question of potentiality is closely related to the theme of agency at the scene of design. Designs shaped by the hegemonic articulation of the technical code will tend to re-enforce the impression that technology is beyond people's control, discouraging non-credentialised people from participation. Feenberg expresses optimism about deepening and extending agency – it is the motor principle of his technical politics. But of particular importance here is the extent to which human individuals now have agency within the technical sphere, and the contrast between this and the situation in other areas of culture. As Feenberg notes, 'despite discouraging developments in other domains, agency in the technical sphere is on the rise' (2010: 55). He associates this with changes to the technical infrastructure itself, writing that in digital culture,

> We are witnessing the end of dystopia as the defining technology of our time shifts from great centralized systems such as electric power and broadcasting to the more loosely structured world of the computer. (Feenberg 2010: 57)

Far from being put off by Laclau and Mouffe's exclusion of systemic properties from the sphere of radical contingency, Feenberg's use of radical democratic theory is to some extent a colonisation of it as well, such is his sense of the importance of technology to contemporary social and political dynamics. He writes, for instance that, 'the social imperatives of capitalism are experienced as technical constraints rather than as political coercion' (2002: 69). This suggests that struggles over the articulation of the technical code are not running in tandem with contests for control of political discourse but actually supplant the significance of the latter. Feenberg is not only saying that he has identified in technology a chink in the armour of the hegemonic system but is also making the stronger claim that it is the only opening available. Traditional politics and even other areas of culture are less important in the dual sense that they do not play the leading role in administering contemporary society and, in contrast to technology, they present no realistic possibilities for active resistance.[18]

4 Moving the boundary of technique

The technical code reifies objects that had previously been open to further determinations and social disputes over their meaning and ultimate form.

This brings them into a chain of equivalences with other technical objects, which ensures they all appear to be technology, with the authoritative presence entailed by that in modern societies.[19] For this to occur under current, capitalist conditions means that any technical object thus constituted contributes to the centralisation of power in a hierarchical social system and enhances the operational autonomy of managers within the production process.

Feenberg emphasises that technology is a dependent social variable, something that is shaped by social activity all the way down: indeed, it is a 'social battlefield' (2002: 15). This activity is always ongoing and dynamic; technological reality is in a permanent condition of flux. As we have seen, for Latour and others, the idea of technology is a contingent product of multiple social situations and nothing more. In other words, it is an idea that may in fact be redundant if the diversity of these situations is such

that it pulls it apart, so to speak. In that circumstance, the idea of technology would simply lose its practical salience and cease to function as
what Latour calls a 'collector' (2013b).

This description of the reality of technology as a process that might
cease to coagulate in a singular social entity comports with Feenberg's
suggestion that technology's essence is thoroughly historical. However,
for critical theory the imposition of discursive identity cannot be
abstracted from questions of social power. The dominant representation of technology is something more than a mere idea, and loosening
its hold is not the straightforward matter that Latour seems to think but
involves social conflicts and political struggle. Technology is a mode
of appearance of objects that has real social consequences, including
those that were the focus of the last chapter. The solidification of technology into the 'material framework of modernity' (Feenberg 2002: 19)
is wrought through social processes, but these are not only linguistic
choices – they reflect the balance of power in society. Reification brings
the contested aspects of any given technology development to an end
and imposes stasis. This fixes its identity and pins it down in relation to
the prevailing idea of technology as such, which includes a prescriptive
sense of what it is for, who may use it, and under what circumstances.

What Feenberg calls 'the boundary of technique' is the inscription
of necessity in technologies: the sense that they must be accepted and
complied with because they embody the 'correct' technical solution.
Whereas in technocracy this boundary was set by large corporations
and few would ever have thought to question a machine beyond learning
how to operate its front end, in recent decades the increased willingness of diverse social agents to challenge technical designs and subvert
authorised patterns of use has created more instability.[20] This change
discloses that 'the boundary of technique is never clear. In fact, identifying that boundary is one of the most important stakes in the struggle
for and against alienated power' (Feenberg 1991: 58–59).

Democratic technical politics aims at shifting the boundary of technique by making more technical practices open to exploration and
experimentation by wider segments of the population. This process,
which Feenberg calls democratic (2002: 92; 2003), subversive (1992) or
sometimes progressive (2017: 220–222) rationalisation, will bring the
operation of established technology more into line with society's needs
and interests. To achieve this, democratic agency has to temporarily de-
reify technology, which must involve 'coding' it in a way that is heteroge-
neous to the technical code as currently constituted.

As seen above, Feenberg gives examples of popular interventions
in the field of technology design that succeed in altering technical
practices and perhaps in displacing the overall meaning of technology.
His suggestion is that activities like this alter the dominant conception of

what technology is, sometimes by restoring a sense of its true purposes. In the example of the patient-activists, the established image of medical experts and scientists in lab coats working in accordance with abstract protocols that laypeople had to respect without really understanding gives way to a more straightforward representation of scientific and technical practices as involving real people making decisions that are consequential for other human beings. In this way, technical-political action breaks down the illusion of technique and replaces it with something more sociologically messy, but also more realistic.

The extent to which agency is now present in the technical sphere means that, for Feenberg, the age of technocracy has passed and it is meaningful to think of 'technical politics'. The process of reification that created technology as a fixed institution is now prone to challenge in the sense that people can discern their own role in producing what counts as technology, and this means that they can make choices that change the technical code, with potentially far-reaching implications for what technology is and what it might become. This is a political radicalisation of the constructivist thesis that different social groups may challenge technology design and that these contests 'shape' the resulting artefacts. It adds to that argument the observation that when they are successful, democratic interventions in technology design can change the meaning of technology by moving the boundary of technique.

As seen in the previous section, according to radical democratic theory, power differentials are the consequence of an ontological contradiction concerning the necessary yet impossible character of society. A social imaginary must be achieved, and yet the social idea can never be finished, completed and stabilised as self-identical. Since it is both utterly necessary for everyone to know that there is a society and objectively quite impossible for them to achieve this, there is an endless struggle to establish institutions, patterns and stability that can retain the confidence of the majority of social subjects. In a sense, they are all compensating for the fundamental lack identified above. This struggle defines the political, and the fact that different groups seek to make theirs the dominant representation makes it agonistic. Feenberg's technical politics, indeed Feenberg's entire dialectic, rests on construing technology, and especially the politics of technology design, on this model.

The point of radical democratic technical politics is to widen the scope for technical interventions by individuals and groups whose current relation to technology is the subordinate one of the worker-user. For them, technology is encountered as something overbearing and authoritative and this is associated, by the hegemonic articulation of the technical code, with its effectiveness. Behind the reified appearance, though, there is real antagonism which technical politics brings into view. Interventions like hacking a communications system, modifying a drug testing regime or demanding better safety standards on industrial machinery break down the illusion of technology as objectively necessary and create new spaces for agency and resistance. In this way they restore a sense of the technical as a locus of antagonism. Once the use and design of technology has been problematised and brought into the realm of meaningful choice for non-expert groups, then the question of social power looms large.

Laclau and Mouffe's theorisation of the political invokes a particular relationship of politics to ontology, which in some ways is highly felicitous for Feenberg's project. Just as constructivism rests its struggles over meaning on the assumption of underdetermination, so technical politics is underscored by the indeterminacy of technical elements, whose concatenation in different designs produces social conflict and competition. Feenberg's contention is that technical politics is an agonistic struggle involving diverse technology users on one side and dominant social interests, especially managers, on the other. The struggle waged by these actors is primarily a struggle over the kind of technology society gets, and is conducted at the scene of design or use, but because technical politics involves breaking down the illusion of technique its ramifications add up to establish the possibility of what Feenberg envisages as a more democratic technology. This would involve moving the boundary of technique to a position consistent with socialist transition.

Progress in technical politics, then, disabuses us of what Feenberg calls the 'technical illusion'. Technology is widely perceived as liberating because it appears to free people in various ways from tricky world-entanglements. While acknowledging the efficacy of technology – it really does solve problems, enable societies to do things differently, achieve more with less effort, etc. – Feenberg emphasises that there is also an illusory element to this. By opening up technical practices to a wider range of social logics, democratic technical politics is a struggle over the dominant representation of technology.

It is clear from this that Feenberg's ontology is not at all the same as the essentialist one of some substantivist philosophers. Technology is whatever it appears to be in any given social formation, but this appearance, Feenberg argues, has a distinctive, albeit illusory, solidity and permanence that qualifies it as 'technology'. As technical infrastructure, technology seems to perdure, to be something more or less immutable, yet at the same time it is a human product susceptible to redesign and even obsolescence and replacement. The illusion of technology's solidity is an instance of reification, in which a human product comes to appear as something alien, powerful and beyond human control. This way of thinking about what technology really is – as contingency that manifests as a certain kind of permanence, somewhere between illusion and reality – comports well with Laclau and Mouffe's negative social ontology.

Technical politics, then, has two layers or aspects, one concerning the war of position over current technical designs, the other more forward-facing and concerned with the place and character of technology in an alternate civilisation. The first lies within the field of articulation as just described, and involves opening up the technical code to diverse social logics that may subvert the hegemonic ordering. The second layer draws on the negative ontological conception of technology with its source in antagonism to identify neglected potential as the basis of a future with a different technical reality. As we will see in the next chapter, this second layer of technology transformation involves an infusion of meaning and value into technical practices.

For Feenberg, the second layer is essential to critique because it is the realisation of human potential for a more meaningful world-relation that connects up the multiple real-world instances of technical politics, from computer hacking to patient activism. These activities are unified through the idea of released potential. Once technology has been opened up to democratic participation, critique faces the question of what it is in any given articulation or 'sort' that connects it to others, and permits the theorist to align them as manifestations of a single counter-hegemonic strategy. The ontological layer of technical politics is Feenberg's framework for answering these questions.

The essence of Feenberg's proposal is that there is a kind of unifying thread that connects such instances of unexpected popular intervention in the previously circumscribed domain of the technical. Ultimately, he believes that interventions like this have the political potential to facilitate the kind of transformation of technology that will add up to wholesale civilisational change. Pursuant to this, he suggests that the meaning of technology has already changed as modern societies have left the 'dystopian' constellation that preoccupied his critical theory forebears. This coincides with digitisation,[21] and the primary result is that the social logics that might articulate the technical code have become more diverse and in consequence its entanglements with other dimensions of social power more complex. The fault-lines, therefore, where contests over technology design and use occur and shape the meaning of technology have also moved. Feenberg acknowledges this, but his model for technical politics remains premised on a confrontation between technological hegemony on one side and potential-releasing, democratic participation on the other.

Feenberg's emphasis on hegemonic technological rationality leads him to posit radical democracy as the privileged counter-value through which space might be created for rival social logics to articulate the technical code. This accommodates a widening of the range of values that might apply to technology design, which makes feasible the kind of civilisational transformation he envisages. However, the new constellation, in which more people are actively shaping technology and technical objects are themselves more active in diverse, unpredictable ways, is different, but it may not take us any closer to machines whose design contributes to a more humanised world.

As we saw in the last chapter Feenberg insists that democratic rationalisation cannot proceed in an instrumental fashion and, equally, that it cannot be a (utopian) matter of wishing nicer machines into existence. Technology holds a distinct structural position in society and has internal protocols that must be respected in any account of the reform process. This means that while design is an important opening for political practice, it must be embedded in an account of wider transformation. While constructivism enables Feenberg to open up the scene of design, so as to think the possibility of people making demands and shaping technologies in a politically motivated direction, he is also wary of the charge of utopianism.[22]

5 Ambiguities of rapid politicisation

Feenberg's idea of the technical code represents a significant advance over earlier versions of constructivism. Without this idea, constructivism cannot account for the persistence of the distinction between technical and non-technical objects, still less explicate what that distinction connotes in contemporary culture. Through it, Feenberg also succeeds in giving renewed political impetus to critical theory, bringing its sense of contradiction and antagonism to the study of a growing arena of political struggle.

The idea of technical politics is, then, a major enhancement to constructivism, giving it a political relevance it otherwise lacks. Feenberg's concept restores the critical tension between technological reality, which is messy and disparate, and the salient conception of technology as something authoritative and final. Where hackers, game modders, social media users, etc. run up against corporate platforms and state controls on internet and technology use, he has identified a burgeoning area of contemporary experience in which critical theory might both gain some traction politically and facilitate a fuller understanding of the meaning of these conflicts.

Using the constructivist insight that technology is socially malleable and susceptible to reform by the power of redescription, Feenberg suggests that it is now the principal medium of political struggle, displacing other forms of public discourse and contested institutions. His examples demonstrate that small-scale technical interventions can have extensive consequences, up to and including effects on the very meaning of technology as a whole – its place and significance in society and culture. In this way, Feenberg redirects critical theory's traditional suspicion of expert discourses into a political opposition of the perspective of ordinary 'users', who for him represent democracy, to those whose technical credentials are a condensation of knowledge (of how things work) and power (over those who only use the things).

Feenberg's work is therefore optimistic about the prospects for democratic reform in the sense that he finds progressive significance in much of what is currently going on and interprets the vibrancy of contemporary techno-culture as confirming his thesis of an emergent technical democracy. There are reasons to be doubtful about this, however. Feenberg's favoured theory of radical democracy might be considered to promote a positive outlook, with lots of activities available to be easily cast as manifestations of democratic resistance because they represent non-compliance with the hegemonic articulation of the technical code. However, if an agonistic model of activity is presupposed, then this may dispose the analyst to find resistance everywhere, especially if the technical has itself been construed as co-terminous with the political.

Earlier versions of critical theory understood the problem of technology in terms of experts using the authority of technology to dictate terms to technology users and, ultimately, imposing an unquestioning compliance on the rest of society. Technical politics is Feenberg's way of thinking through openings that have ruptured this scenario, and democracy is an important value in that process. However, with the change of cultural horizon involved in breaking with dystopia, technology has already shed its association with the unquestionable authority of experts, or even with narrow efficiency as a goal. The diffusion of digital technologies has encouraged the development of diverse cultures of experimentation, dabbling, reconfiguring, sabotage and so on. To the extent that the Internet, for instance, is a place where everyone periodically plays with technology, and mobile phones have become toys that people trust and incorporate into every aspect of their lives, what Feenberg calls the technical illusion has already evaporated.

Much of this activity would have been unthinkable just a few decades ago, and this must be at least partly attributed to the fact that technology now exists in networks that extend into places not primarily associated with work and control. These networks produce and are produced by articulations of the technical code that are embedded in cultural values like play and learning, rather than control or efficiency. Technology is as likely to be held equivalent to things that can be trusted, that are life-enhancing, individual, even eccentric, as it is to be associated with corporate power or government control.

This is not to say that the technical code has lost its connection with social domination. On the contrary, the entwinement of technology's network with those of social power seems to be as profound and pervasive in its consequences as ever. Under this changed cultural horizon, however, the technical code is no longer subject to one or two kinds of articulation. Feenberg himself makes this point when he writes that 'technical rationality consists of various loosely related dimensions with different social implications' (1991: 178), but he does not draw the necessary conclusion for technical politics from this observation. If diverse rationalities are present in technology, then the competing values at stake are also already multiple rather than binary.

The usefulness of the technical code idea is compromised by Feenberg's imposition of a binary political battle concept onto it. His conception of technical politics as an agonistic struggle between democracy and hegemonic technological rationality effaces sociological and political details that are, in consequence, left out of account in the theory of technical politics. As we have seen in this chapter, Feenberg's claim that technology is the principal or even the only vehicle of hegemonic power in contemporary society even threatens the wider theory of radical democracy with absorption into technical politics. His assertion that the technical code is *the* vehicle of contemporary hegemony may be a feature of theories, like Laclau and Mouffe's version of radical democracy, that rest on negative ontological foundations. A fundamental antagonism defines the field and gives it its agonistic structure, but it also seems to entail that other fields cannot also be fundamental.

Lois McNay has argued that this kind of overreach is a pervasive feature of theories she characterises as pre-emptively motivated to present aspects of social reality as political. In her critique of Mouffe's work in particular, McNay argues that 'the logic of social being exceeds the explanatory force of the one-dimensional antagonistic logic of signification' (2014: 8). In other words, those processes that stand beyond the reach of political discourse are not merely amorphous, or the locus of an unrepresentable antagonism, but reflect the presence of important dimensions of social reality studied by other disciplines. She points out that social processes, including those involving symbolic violence, recede in radical democratic theory to become an undifferentiated 'blob', obscured by the overbearing, fascinating logic of the political.

In this respect technical politics mirrors radical democracy's 'linguistic universalism' (McNay 2014: 18), assuming that everyone is involved with technology in much the same way that Laclau and Mouffe assume everyone would have the capacity to participate in political speech, were it not for the way that politics is currently structured. The under-representation of social groups (women, some ethnic groups, people with some disabilities) in technical professions is a long-standing concern of sociologists of technology (Wacjman 2004). Technical politics neglects to include any space for the multiple *social* causes of their marginality. Instead their exclusion is viewed solely as one of the negative consequences of hegemonic technological rationality, perpetrated by formal bias in technology design. This fails to address the exclusion of groups of people who never encounter a codified technical object, some of whom decide at an early age that technology is 'not for them', perhaps as a result of internalising a sense of inferiority to experts and knowledgeable men. Sociological processes that limit and inhibit women's interest in technology, for example, are not themselves reducible to the codification of technology as male – it is one factor among many, and it needs to be understood through a wider, sociological lens. The danger here may be that in rushing to conceive technology as politics, critical theory fails to challenge the fine-grained, social processes through which privileged forms of access and technical control are reproduced, or to accommodate any account of the social processes through which those who are excluded from a role in technology might thematise their exclusion, gain recognition for it and turn it into a political issue.

If Feenberg's use of radical democratic theory effaces sociological questions around human agency, it also obscures the active, substantive role of specific technologies, which also tend to be viewed in binary terms either as threats, because they instantiate the hegemonic technological rationality, or as signs of an as yet quite abstract potentiality. Feenberg's thought remains conservative in this sense. While it might be expected that democratic challenges to capitalist hegemony would create openings for new ideas and designs that embody different values, his discussion of the latter never strays beyond recurrent reference to the notion of a currently neglected potentiality. The social (ontological) reality of technology, he argues, is matched by an idea of latent human or social potential. He writes that 'it is important to retain a strong notion of potentiality with which to challenge existing designs' (2002: 33), but this allusion to potential is as far as the theory goes in projecting an alternative version of the technical code.

The question of potential brings us to a further problem with the theory as currently formulated, which is that the benefits of democratisation are nearly always presented as essentially *negative*, or defensive. As we saw in the last chapter, Feenberg opposes conservative strategies aimed at containment of technology from positions in culture outside technology (for example, restrictions on embryo research), yet he is equally clear that the primary beneficial consequence of democratisation will consist in checking certain kinds of technology design from within. This might seem to betray an ongoing concern with technology as a threat, reflecting Feenberg's belief that current technology is a reified version, shaped by capitalist interests. Defining technology as a social process, he envisages democracy as a restraining force within technology design, holding negative developments back, rather than an externally imposed cultural constraint. However, while inhibiting hegemonic distortions from within in this way is, perhaps, a necessary first step, it is not clear that installing cultural constraints as internal to the design process is a sufficient condition for further progressive change.

If Feenberg is evasive on the nature of this positive potential, he exaggerates the extent to which the multiple interventions that constitute democratic rationalisation really are internally connected as manifestations of progress, with the overarching implications for the system that he ascribes to them. It is not clear that subversions of established uses of technology are always steps towards democracy, even when they improve the lives of specific groups of individuals. Patient activism has shortened the time spent testing new drugs and saved lives, but it is questionable whether it amounts to, or even contributes to, progress in any wider sense. A popular challenge to expertise cannot be considered a step in a progressive direction merely because it questions technical authority, illustrated by the fact that Europe and North America are currently in the midst of a measles epidemic, perhaps partly caused by popular scepticism about vaccinations.

Similarly, computer hackers have shifted the boundary of technique in the sense that they have promoted the idea of the computer network as something non-expert people may use as a medium of self-expression, but the sociology of this does not involve enhancements to democracy. Instead, the diffusion of accessible networked computing has been associated with the emergence of cultures (such as those associated with hacking and gaming) in which informal hierarchies of expertise and patterns of social exclusion are rigidly and often aggressively enforced. These developments have been associated with criminal organisations' use of networks and, partly in consequence, with repressive legislation that criminalises certain forms of computer use (Chandler 1996) and constructs a new, normativised conception of the 'user'. It is true that in the digital era, customising technology and shaping it to one's own requirements has become a normal part of life for perhaps the majority of people. However, inequalities persist and proliferate within this culture of diffuse technical know-how, and there has been no corresponding progressive change that might merit description as 'democratisation'.

Democracy, it seems, does not play the transformative role in technical politics that Feenberg assigns to it, even if popular interventions of the kind he identifies do create space for alternative values which might shape the technical code of the future. Moreover, when it has been applied to technical systems democracy has not always led to their ethical improvement when viewed in historical perspective. There is no easy association of democratisation with the ethics (or aesthetics) of a superior civilisational model. Feenberg envisages 'mutually supporting transformations' (2002: 27) as if they were a natural consequence of loosening the grip of the technical code. But numerous examples, such as the practice of eugenics in Sweden in the 1970s, suggest that the finest democracy can go together with abusive medical (and other) technologies. Perhaps the underlying problem here is that the very conditions that make democratising technology design thinkable also vitiate any notion of progress: in pure democracy the future has no direction aside from the one people choose to give it.

It is perhaps for this reason that Feenberg approaches the notion of a future technical code with a degree of caution. There is inconsistency between the idea of technical politics as an open-ended play of articulations, widening the circle of included participants while always struggling against hegemony (against a background of antagonism), and Feenberg's Marcusean orientation towards reconciliation and harmony (with something like Marx's 'end of history' providing a sense of direction). Perhaps the multiple struggles over technologies and the changes they bring about do not add up to anything like progress in the Marcusean sense. This probably depends on the kinds of values that get imposed on technology and the extent to which they finesse Feenberg's notion of potential. The next two chapters address this.

Notes

1 'Manual' here is a placeholder for the authority that guides users in their initial engagements with machines and other artefacts. It includes instructions from the boss at work, conventions and patterns of use sedimented in the bodies of workers as habits, and even visual metaphors in a graphical user interface.

2 The idea of hegemony antedates Gramsci's intervention, though the latter has become the definitive point of reference. Perry Anderson traces the origins of the modern concept to nineteenth-century debates over nationalism and the state, where it signifies the role of a unifying power, and notes that with Gramsci's intervention, 'hegemony … acquired two enlargements of meaning in tension with each other. It now included both the extraction by rulers of consent from the ruled, and the deployment of coercion to enforce their rule' (Anderson 2017: 21).

3 This does not mean he was any less perceptive a critic of the negative effects of reification on psychological and cultural life. As Boggs puts it, 'Gramsci pointed to Taylorism in the US and the fascist corporate state in Italy as harbingers of the most sophisticated mode of capitalist domination, in which workers would be totally subordinated to machine specialization and the cult of efficiency. The diffusion of bureaucratic-technological norms would mean the destruction of all intellectual, artistic, and even human content to production and, in the end the grinding down of the workers' life to virtual nothingness' (1976: 47). Gramsci refers to the spread of psychoanalysis as a symptom of 'the increased moral coercion exercised by the apparatus of State and society on single individuals, and of the pathological crisis determined by this coercion' (1982: 280).

4 The affinity with reification is clear when Gramsci writes that 'One of the commonest totems is the belief about everything that exists, that it is "natural" that it should exist ... and that however badly one's attempts to reform may go they will not stop life going on, since the traditional forces will continue to operate and precisely will keep life going on ... One may say that no real movement becomes aware of its global character all at once, but only gradually through experience – in other words when it learns from the facts that nothing which exists is natural ... but rather exists because of certain conditions' (cited in Boggs 1976: 110).

5 In his *Prison Notebooks*, which were scrutinised by a fascist censor, Gramsci's phrase for Marxism was 'the philosophy of praxis' (Gramsci 1982). A similar emphasis on praxis is found in other Hegel-inspired Marxist scholarship, such as the work of Karl Korsch (1970) and, of course, Georg Lukàcs (1981). Steven Vogel (in Arnold and Michel 2017) provides an interesting discussion of the epistemic function of praxis in Feenberg's thought.

6 Even Marcuse's notion of a new technics as the exit point from one-dimensional society is suggestive of a social imaginary in which technology and technologists play a controlling role.

7 This point is emphasised in some constructivist studies. For example, Bowker and Starr suggest that 'classifications and standards are *material* as well as symbolic' (1999: 39). It tends to be assumed that the two aspects are inseparable: motivated relabelling drives physical amendment and substantive alteration is reflected in changes of terminology.

8 'Technology must really work. But it is not merely because a device works that it is chosen for development over many other equally coherent configurations of technical elements' (Feenberg 2002: 79).

9 'The more one studies technological arrangements, the more one considers their ins and outs, the less chance one has of unifying them in a coherent whole' (Latour 2013b: 213).

10 Wiebe Bijker acknowledges that in most constructivist scholarship there is a 'missing link' between these details and the question of power (1997: 261). It is this link that Feenberg's idea of a technical code tries to provide.

11 Feenberg refers to a scale of meaningfulness for technological artefacts, ranging from 'semantic impoverishment' to 'richest object relations' (2010: 175).

12 In this it corresponds to what Bowker and Star describe as a classification system, forming 'a juncture of social organization, moral order, and layers of technical integration' (Bowker and Star 1999: 33).

13 And all other practices: their theory has been accused of 'absolutising' language (Geras 1987), in common with its post-structuralist sources.

14 'To enumerate is never an innocent operation; it involves major displacements of meaning' (Laclau and Mouffe 1985: 62–63).

15 'The hegemonic form of politics only becomes dominant at the beginning of modern times, when the reproduction of the different social areas takes place by permanently changing conditions which constantly require the constitution of new systems of differences' (Laclau and Mouffe 1985: 138).

16 Laclau and Mouffe write that in 'industrial society there is a growing unification of the social terrain around the image of the mechanism' (1985: 36), which perhaps reflects the hold of a particular hegemonic conception of technology

on their thought and surely represents a regression behind Gramsci's insights, cited above.

17 Allan Dreyer Hansen usefully describes Laclau and Mouffe's theory in the following terms: 'Discourse theory's ontology consists in a set of limits and *im*possibilities, and its theorizing is based on these. It starts from the basic claim of the "impossibility of society" and the essential unfixity of all possible social objects. Society is impossible because it is "haunted" by an unsurmountable negativity ... which cannot be sublated in any dialectical movement ... Radical negativity means that it cannot be positivised by a deeper objectivity (e.g. the cunning of reason, society's movement of stages towards communism, etc.)' (2014: 286).

18 Feenberg writes that 'natural science and technology define the framework of capitalist civilization after World War II' (2002: 167), and that nothing less than 'the meaning of modernity is at stake' in technical politics (2002: 114). He also emphasises that human beings are now *in* technology – that is, immersed in a technological environment and shaped by it to a new, unprecedented extent.

19 It should be noted that the integration of new technologies into this system of representation is not often seamless. New technologies tend to destabilise what technology means, with implications for associated power structures. Feenberg writes that 'new technology can threaten the hegemony of the ruling groups until it has been strategically encoded' (2002: 79). After that, however, once it has received the technical code, 'everywhere technology goes, centralized, hierarchical social structures follow' (2002: 24).

20 Latour is the ideologist of this tendency: he abstracts it from questions of social power and presents the dissolution of technological hegemony as if it has already happened.

21 Relatively early in the digital transition, Feenberg observed that 'it matters what we do about technology because, perhaps for the first time in history, public involvement is beginning to have significant impact on the shape of technological change' (1995: 2).

22 Marcuse was famously accused by Habermas (1989) of naively recommending a dialogue with nature because he moved too quickly in developing his vision/ fantasy of a radically different technology.

4

Aesthetic critique

Feenberg draws on the insights of social constructivism to argue that the design of technologies is a contentious, disputed and thoroughly political process. Technologies come heavily inscribed with symbolic meanings, including, in capitalist society, the message that they are authoritative and determinate. One of Feenberg's innovations has been to show how these social inscriptions not only construct technology in line with the conceptions of specific social groups but, at the same time, tie artefacts into wider social networks (2010: 76). Enlarging the picture in this way reveals that, as a social process, creating and shaping technologies is not bracketed off from other practices but always closely entwined with them. It also suggests that the symbolic inscription of technical artefacts is a richer process than the mere communication of function to putative users: here too there is a politics, which Feenberg understands in terms of aestheticisation.

Feenberg politicises technology design not by reducing the process to purportedly more profound layers of the social formation (which was, perhaps, the old Marxist way of achieving the same thing) but by demonstrating the connection between technology and social power as this is manifest in the technical code. An object is recognisable as technology precisely when and because it bears certain significations that speak of (and to) wider social relations: it is efficient; it is an enhancement to what was done previously; it represents the future; and so on. These things are written into the symbolic aspect of the artefact along with the specific instructions on its operation, concerning which tasks it performs and what problems it solves, on its user interface. These inscriptions make it recognisable as technology and, in so doing, they position it in a wider web of social meanings and values. None of the latter (efficiency, the future) are specific to technology, but in modern society they are integral to its meaning and to prevailing notions of what technology 'is'.

This chapter explores Feenberg's argument that modern technology stands in need of 're-aestheticisation'. Aesthetic critique connects the political analysis of specific contexts of social shaping to the wider goal of civilisational change. As indicated in the previous chapter, there is a theoretical difficulty in connecting the ontic concerns of politicised constructivism to such a wider project of transformation, which seems to be ontological in its implications. Feenberg's conception of aesthetic critique serves as the normative linchpin that connects these two parts of the theory. Progressive re-articulations of the technical code result in alternative concatenations of technical elements in designs that are superior because they serve more people's interests more effectively than capitalist ones. Aesthetic critique adds to this the idea that progressive reinscriptions also have consequences that extend beyond practical alterations to the performance of the technology, to change the values operative in technology design and thereby alter the meaning of technology as a social institution.

Feenberg argues that there is an inherent affinity between progressive technical politics and the aesthetics of naturalistic modernism, and that design changes inspired by this association will bring about the kind of profound cultural transformation necessary to take us forward to a superior civilisational model. This part of his argument rests on an organicist, holistic approach to social totality, in which reconciliation of the human with nature and technology, fulfilled in part by technology that humanises nature, are key values. I will suggest that on this point Feenberg's argument has been historically superseded. Precisely the kind of aesthetic modernism he recommends is now hegemonic in contemporary design, and it has not brought about any progressive advance in terms of economic justice or democratic politics. Notwithstanding this, both the notion of an aesthetic critique and the political significance assigned to it are important to Feenberg's overall advance in relation to other varieties of constructivism or rival critical approaches to technology. The chapter recommends a modified version of aesthetic critique that is based on difference rather than wholeness, and on the principle that there is no inherent correspondence of aesthetic standards with the ethics immanent to technology design.

The aesthetic aspects of design are an important issue at stake between different constituencies who seek to make artefacts comport with their definitions of technology and what it is for. Aesthetic critique addresses the sedimentation of values associated with past technologies (and their codifications) in the foundations of contemporary cultural life. If democratising the scene of technology design allows user groups and workers a voice in shaping machines that are more pleasant to work with, this aesthetic dimension also bears upon the attempt to reposition technology in wider webs of meaning.

There is a connection here with environmentalism and movements that sometimes appear to be 'anti-technology' in their orientation. When he discusses this aspect of aesthetic critique, Feenberg often refers to essentialist critics of technology (especially Heidegger and Marcuse), for whom the question of civilisation change, predicated on the development of a radically different kind of technical infrastructure, was a key concern. The notion of aesthetic critique is the bridge in Feenberg's theory between his embrace of constructivism, with its emphasis on contingency and local, contemporary struggles, and his attachment to the long-term historical concerns of such essentialist philosophies of technology. Feenberg has stated that the normative or critical imperatives of his theory are in fact grounded here, writing that 'aesthetics provides the normative basis for the reconstruction of technological rationality' (Feenberg 2005: xv).

Section 1 places Feenberg's ideas about aesthetics in the context of his technical politics, positioning them within his critical version of constructivism as part of the codification of technology – a process that includes technology's 'neutral' appearance as a decisive outcome. This relates to the question of the aesthetics of technology as the focus of a kind of locally initiated reform that might herald wider changes with implications for the character of civilisation. Section 2 positions aesthetic critique thus defined at the intersection of constructivism and traditional critical theory, where it carries the values of a wider project oriented to civilisation change and makes it possible to bring them to bear upon contemporary technology designs while evading the charge of utopianism, or flouting the rationality conditions that must preside over technical thinking.

Section 3 describes the thesis of re-aestheticisation of capitalist technology with reference to Feenberg's argument that all technology includes what he calls primary and secondary 'instrumentalisation'. The first of these involves an originary violence, without which there can be no technology, while the second is restorative and compensates nature by mediating the result through symbolic meaning. In capitalist societies the second of these moments is stymied, resulting in a cold, one-dimensional technology and a correspondingly shallow way of life. Here, Feenberg's notion of an aesthetic dimension re-presents Marcuse's thesis of an enlarged or transformed mode of technical reasoning, compatible with a new kind of civilisation. I question whether the idea of an aesthetic transformation can bear the weight of these essentially utopian ideas and, in the concluding section, recommend an alternative understanding of the place of the aesthetic in contemporary technical politics, drawing on ideas from elsewhere in Feenberg's work and the critical theory tradition.

1 Aesthetics in technical politics

In presenting technology as a phenomenon of social connection, Feenberg stresses that he is making an anti-essentialist move. As we have seen, he argues that 'technology is a dependent variable in the social system, shaped to a purpose by the dominant class and subject to reshaping to new purposes under a new hegemony' (Feenberg 1991: 35). The importance of such a definition is multiple. It is historically accurate, because people have not always talked about technology in the same ways that they do today. It is important to register differences like the foregrounding of the word 'technology', which happens in English in the eighteenth century, for example, and heralds a relatively recent framing of devices and machines, which were previously described as various 'mechanical arts' (Jennings 1985; Adas 1989). In contrast, the essentialist view illegitimately projects back contemporary meanings to establish a connection among proto-tools used by monkeys, medieval sewing implements and nuclear power stations, as if they were all manifestations of the same, continuous phenomenon. This underestimates the contingency that really attaches to technology and other social practices, supporting narratives (from socio-biology to optimistic visions of progress) that obscure the real, underdetermined[1] nature of technology design.

This relational definition marks a cutting loose from ways of thinking that place large investments in particular narrative constructions on technology as a long-standing yet dynamic dimension of the human story. For example, Marx presented technology as both the outcome of local projects rooted in specific social conflicts and one of the cornerstones of human economic development. As discussed in Chapter 1, he states in a number of places that capitalist technology is shaped to facilitate the domination of workers (e.g. Marx 1990: 562), while, at the same time, he identifies technology as historically continuous and even discusses its origins in hunting and war (1990: 452). For Marx, human history is the growth of productive power – the expansion of the productive forces, which includes technology – and this strongly implies some kind of progress, from inferior tools of previous modes of production to the advanced machines of capitalism that will ultimately set us free (e.g. Marx 1981: 701).

Feenberg's position on what technology is and on its social-relational character is intended to be consistent with Marx's vision of human self-realisation, but it also involves a careful uncoupling of technology from the long-term, uni-directional vision of historical materialism. Feenberg doesn't want to abandon the connection with Marx, or the idea that history may exhibit a progressive pattern in which technology plays an important part. His advocacy of an idea of historical advance, or progress, is crucial because it is part of what puts the 'critical' into critical theory and, as such, makes Feenberg more than just another constructivist.[2] However, retaining this notion while doing justice to local disputes over the meanings of specific technologies is no easy matter. Feenberg has to be faithful to the meaning-assignments of proximal social agents while at the same time maintaining a connection between them and wider struggles with a higher-order significance that are often only appreciated by social actors elsewhere in historical time.[3]

Marx provided detailed accounts of social struggle and more than one statement of his theory of history, but he had less to say about the cultural mediations of meaning that occur in a society in which technology is increasingly salient in experience. Following in the footsteps of earlier critical theorists, Feenberg identifies Max Weber's work on societal rationalisation, but also Heidegger's critique of modern technology and Marcuse's vision of 'civilizational transformation', to expand Marx's theory. Part of Feenberg's project is to try and maintain a connection between these conceptions of the meaning of technology in modern culture and fine-grained accounts of struggles over technology design, in an account of historical change. At stake in the local struggles described by constructivists, he maintains, is the issue of what technology means in a global sense, and this has a bearing on the kind of society that will exist in the future.

Constructivist scholars have provided detailed descriptive histories of struggles over the meanings of individual technologies, but they have been accused of abstracting them from wider social relationships. Langdon Winner (1993), in particular, points out that constructivism seems to be blind both to the contexts that condition actors' interests in a given technology and to the wider consequences of their struggles. Feenberg's theory brings relationality and connectedness. He shows that the scene of technology design is always already pre-coded as technical, meaning that some actors will be empowered as 'experts' and (normally) that in this designation, knowledge is condensed with the representation of dominant social interests. Moreover, the imprint that products bear as technologies ensures that they will be perceived as 'neutral' at the end of these social processes. The 'technical code' in modern societies emphasises that technology is value-free and only present in the workplace because it enhances efficiency. This appearance of neutrality – of technology as the objective solution to a problem – is vital to understanding how technology comports with social power.

As discussed in Chapter 2, Feenberg maintains that, like other formal systems associated with modernity (bureaucracy, public law), technology presents as free of substantive entanglements or biases. Technology does not seem to favour any particular social group, and it does not make arguments for this or that point of view. The common perception of technology is that it is not subject to moral questioning: if someone chooses to set it to a 'bad' purpose then it is the person and not the machine that is at fault. Technical artefacts are made to appear as somehow above the political fray of further contestation and dispute. The production of this reified appearance masks the disputed design decisions while ensuring that all parties, including the people who have to live with the consequences, accept that it is the best design because it is the most efficient. As such, the codification of technology as 'neutral' is a necessary, critical supplement to the constructivist idea of 'closure'.[4]

Feenberg's politicisation of constructivism involves using its methods to reopen the historical questions that are placed out of view by this neutral codification in order to make social actors aware that they can challenge individual technical designs and bring their own interests and values to bear upon them.[5] Feenberg deconstructs technology's codification as 'neutral' by reading this appearance both as an instance of reification and as a variety of discourse in Foucault's sense of the term. Viewed in this way, technology resembles stretches of language that represent *and* constitute the world for agents, who must find margins of manoeuvre within the interstices of authoritative sense-making and associated institutionalised forms of domination. Foucault's rhetorics to one side,[6] it is clear that real material technologies often dovetail with stratagems of power – one thinks of the physical design of prisons, or of psycho-pharmacology – and reference to this enables Feenberg to suggest that technology itself functions like a discourse, as well as operating adjacent to it.

Feenberg's technical politics distinguishes between strategic implementations of technology that both serve dominant interests and re-enforce the dominant codification of it as a neutral structure, and tactical operations on the part of resisting subjects. The latter grapple with metaphoric 'technics of domination', but also with real machinery and technologies that establish procedurally correct behavioural templates and, in so doing, leave behind spaces for subversion. In the case of technology designs, these spaces are occupied wherever social groups come together and demand something better from established technical means. The patients' groups who oblige medical authorities to speed up drug testing, for example, are engaged in a kind of Foucauldian counter-practice[7] that tries to reshape spaces previously sculpted exclusively by experts. Technical politics, then, accounts for the appearance of technology's neutrality as the outcome of social processes and a determinate codification of technical artefacts, *and* it specifies a way in which this might be challenged. Each time a technology design is subjected to democratic challenge, it both improves that technology and, potentially at least, changes the global meaning of technology as well.

Feenberg's theory suggests that local struggles to reopen technology designs and challenge their objectivity create at the same time openings to a larger, wider kind of change involving the meaning of technology itself and associated with civilisational change. This marks an opening to the critical theory tradition, and its raising of larger questions. If modern technology's appearance of neutral efficiency is contingent on social processes, what are the implications for social change? Might a technology be envisaged in which the particular and the sensuous are foregrounded in the human experience of artefacts – one in which the term 'technology' no longer serves as a connector linking all of its instances and associating them with other sources of neutral authority? This brings us to the aesthetic dimension of the theory.

2 Marcuse, aesthetics and critique

Herbert Marcuse was the Frankfurt School theorist most preoccupied with technocracy, a social system defined by its effacement of democracy in deference to the rule of technical imperatives, usually implemented by experts. Positive advocates of technocracy, of which there have been few, recommend finding technical solutions to human problems and implementing them in systems that are as efficient as possible without regard for the feelings or opinions of affected social subjects, which are treated as potential negative feedback to be managed by the system. According to technocracy, expertise ought to be authoritative and able to circumvent communicative or deliberative procedures aimed at securing democratic legitimation. Technocracy was often the implicit, dystopic situation for the first generation of critical theorists because it represented the clearest formulation of a society whose sole organising principle was a narrowly construed rationality, resulting in a society so irrational no one would choose to live in it.

Although his work allowed greater scope for political action than that of other Frankfurt School theorists, Marcuse's critique of technocracy was, like theirs, aesthetically grounded (Marcuse 1978). He objected to the narrow emphasis on function over other concerns in capitalist machines, and associated this with the technocratic corrosion of meaning in modern life. His aesthetic critique traced these developments to the separation of function and form that distinguished capitalist technology. Historically, tools and artefacts had combined a concern with effectiveness with an interest in enhancing the quality of lived human experience. In pre-capitalist societies, technology's aesthetic – what it was like in a qualitative sense – was not separate or subordinate to quantitative measures of its performance but unified in a common purpose of making the world more amenable. Capitalist technology reflects (and imposes) a different logic, according to which the prioritisation of function and efficiency over what things feel like to use is partly constitutive of technology. This separation corresponds to a profound division within the human psyche, established in the sixteenth and seventeenth centuries.

The modern period saw the emergence of a mode of subjectivity that was premised on distinguishing reality, which was ordered and comprehensible using ratiocination and calculative procedures, from fantasy, which is the realm of imagination. A subject structured in this way is both a basic outcome of modern social processes and a fundamental condition for modernity, including modern technology. The corresponding objective world is inert and neutral, yet also opaque and threatening. This conception of subject and object as both internally divided and mutually opposed is a founding condition of modernity as understood by critical theory. Critique is motivated by the sense that these splits, while historically necessary, might be overcome in a society based on reconciliation and harmony between the multiple elements. The hope that this might be so is carried by experience itself, which is always richer and runs in excess of the epistemic limits set by this foundation.

For example, external nature is experienced as 'more' than just stuff to be used by people who, on some level, know themselves to be more than just functional cogs in a machine for which their emotions and sensuous responses are at best mere lubricants. Critical theory draws on the analysis of experience, then, to find out this 'more' and direct it against the alienating effects of the system. Consequently, critical theorists are particularly interested in the aesthetic – what the world feels like to humans – and in the ways that this poses a challenge to the dominant codification of life in a 'rationalised' society.

The belief that a different model of selfhood would be necessary for socialist civilisation was fundamental to socialist thinking in the twentieth century, including, for example, the Soviet project of the 'new person', who is virtuous because they subordinate their own interests to the production requirements of society as a whole. Marcuse gives the idea of a new kind of human a distinctive, Freudian spin by envisaging the reintegration of the reality and pleasure principles in a new subjectivity (Marcuse 1961). This would result in subjects for whom the objective natural world is not a mere resource to be used, but a realm of sensuous, potentially meaningful experiences, while the imagination is not restricted to art and literature but recognised as playing an active role in making sense of the world.

This reintegration of the human sense of reality with the powers of imagination sounds esoteric, but its influence on Feenberg is important. I suggested in Chapter 2 that the immanent ethics of technology design, central to Feenberg's approach, rests upon an implicit thesis that technology is motivated by the urge to improve life for human beings.

Similarly, for all that technology increasingly relies on abstract know-ledge about materials and so on, it also needs ideas and imagination: in this sense, technology is unthinkable without reference to the fantastic, and its historical development can be described as a process in which imagination has transformed the world. In common with other critical theorists, Marcuse suggests that this transformation has gone off course in the modern period, in part because it has lost connection with its own fundamental mission:

> Only if the vast capabilities of science and technology, of the scien-tific and artistic imagination direct the construction of a sensuous environment, only if the work world loses its alienating features and becomes a world of human relationships, only if productivity becomes creativity, are the roots of domination dried up in the individuals. No return to precapitalist, pre-industrial artisanship, but on the contrary, perfection of the new mutilated and distorted science and technology in the formation of the object world in accordance with 'the laws of beauty'. And 'beauty' here defines an ontological condition – not of an *oeuvre d'art* isolated from real existence ... but that harmony between man and his world which would shape the form of society. (Cited in Feenberg 2008: 1)

The suggestion that reason itself might recuperate technology, setting it right again from within, is based on a very specific notion of reconcili-ation, in which technology, nature and the human subject are all funda-mentally reconfigured.

Marcuse envisaged a new technology that would reflect an influx of imagination into its design and reveal a new world in which the free play of the faculties, not only efficiency, becomes part of what people expect from technics. This transformation would dissociate technology from the struggle for survival that has been artificially prolonged by capitalism and connect it with the fulfilment of human desires. Instead of technology to dominate and control nature, Marcuse imagined technics that would be 'designed and utilized for the pacification of the struggle for existence' (1964: 227). Such technology would be aesthetic 'to the degree to which the productive machinery is constructed with a view of the free play of faculties' (1964: 240), while imagination becomes synonymous with tech-nology: 'In the light of the capabilities of advanced industrial civilization', Marcuse asked, 'is not all play of the imagination playing with technical possibilities?' (1964: 249). For him, a redesigned technology could be the basis for a constellation in which humanity, nature and artefacts would be reconciled in a softer, more humanised world.

This part of Marcuse's theory was famously criticised by Jürgen Habermas (1989), who accused him of seeking to establish a society based on dialogue with nature. The suggestion was that Marcuse was some-thing of 'a dreamer' (Feenberg 2005: 100). In contrast, Habermas (1985) argued that modern technology is a gain of societal evolution, reflecting the progressive differentiation of the systems sphere, which handles our relations with a nature that is not susceptible to persuasion. Feenberg counters that this view of technology is no less unrealistic than Marcuse's and alleges that Habermas writes as if technology wasn't implicated in environmental degradation and dehumanising work practices, effectively idealising it as an agent of social progress.

In contrast, Feenberg praises Marcuse's vision because it 'calls for change in the very nature of technological rationality' (2005: 98),[8] and he takes over the idea of an aesthetic revolution in technology design. He rejects any retreat from Marcuse's objective of total trans- formation in the 'meaning' of technology as a regression behind basic insights of Heidegger. For Feenberg, if we can't have a dialogue with nature, we are not necessarily committed to being at war with it either. Acknowledging that Marcuse lacked any account of how his vision of reconciliation might be implemented in practice, Feenberg presents his own technical politics as providing conceptual resources to fill this gap. The hegemony of modern technology's rationality need not be overturned 'all at once'. In place of essentialist critique based on the possibility of a new 'world-revealing', a politicised construct- ivism with an aesthetic dimension can serve as a better standpoint for comprehending the fundamental categorial reorderings that are neces- sary to develop what he, following Marcuse, envisages as a change of civilisational proportions.

At important moments in his elaboration of the aesthetic as a ground for the technical politics that mediate this change, Feenberg invokes an idea of resonance or harmony between the way that humans apprehend the world and an objective reality that is 'out there', so to speak, to be experienced. For example, in his account of Marcuse's theory, Feenberg refers to 'consensual notions of beauty', and to 'natural harmonies' (2005: 109) between humanity and nature that exceed scientific explan- ation, even though they are present in things like scientists' preference for elegant mathematical demonstrations (2005: 107). The aesthetic demand for a technology that comports with inner and outer nature and seeks harmony between them is, on Feenberg's reading of Marcuse's theory, a matter of meaning, specifically of an influx of previously neglected values into technology design and a corresponding alteration to the symbolic mediation characteristic of technical practices. For Feenberg the aes- thetic dimension is central to the critical theory of technology because, far from being a superficial matter about the appearance of machinery, it concerns technology's role in mediating the rest of human experi- ence. Changing technology design to include a different set of aesthetic principles will alter its experiential character and ultimately reposition it in a new constellation of humanity, objects and nature.

Feenberg acknowledges that the starting point for this aesthetic critique cannot consist in a fixed idea of human nature but must be grounded historically and relationally. To this end, he retrieves from the young Marx the notion that our sensory apparatus may itself be subject to historically (that is, not biologically) driven variations over the course of the historical process: there is a 'historical biology' of sense perception (2005: 120–121). Drawing on this idea, he proposes to develop his aesthetic critique through a phenomenological account of the resonances humans can find in the world at any given point. On this basis, he says, we can have access to the gains associated with ontological critique – namely, a perspective in which technology mediates our world-relations in very different ways under various historical circumstances – without the essentialist connotations of full-blown Heideggerianism (according to which technology in the modern sense would be associated with a negative enframing and contrasted with an entirely different, more authentic, yet long-lost and barely accessible world-revealing).

In aesthetic critique, then, the variability to be uncovered and used to highlight the contingent character of current 'truths' (about technology, its 'correct' form as the one that is 'most efficient', etc.) remains thoroughly historical, has to be elaborated phenomenologically[9] and can be directly articulated to technical-political projects, where it might even serve as a kind of critical index on the ambition of specific reform proposals relative to the goal of civilisation change. Here Feenberg recasts Marcuse's notion of a reformed 'technological rationality' as a matter of introducing variation into the technical code, which he hopes will give the idea of aesthetic reform 'a more concrete sociological element' (2005: 104). He retains from Marcuse, however, commitment to a particular conception of progressive change as involving a restoration of natural harmonies or reintegration of societal elements thought of as part of an organic whole.[10]

Moreover, there are dangers in any such project of reconciliation, perhaps especially when it is to be politically mediated. Part of the motivation for Habermas's repudiation of Marcuse lay in a concern about the potentially totalitarian implications of a politics based on renouncing reason and incorporating feelings into political debate. Theodor Adorno also refused Marcuse's Freudian formula for a better world. The danger courted by theories of a new subjectivity in which perception and fantasy co-mingle in a modified reality principle is that of moving from the present irrational rationality to a potentially worse irrational irrationality. While it is clear that the current dispensation favours a narrow, even paranoid world-relation, it remains impossible using the resources of speculative theory alone to specify a superior one in advance. As Espen Hamer points out, this dilemma leads Adorno to favour a version of Kantian autonomy over any such prescriptive model for future reconciliation.[11] Adorno's approach focuses on non-identity, and his analysis of experience seeks out moments of resistance to power's reduction of the subject to its representation, or to self-identity.

However, Feenberg contends that Adorno, whose work he compares unfavourably with Marcuse's on this point, regresses behind Kant when he offers an aesthetics based on mediated non-identity (Feenberg 2005: 117–118). Feenberg also casts this position as an evasion on Adorno's part (2005: 118–119), because it maintains the non-identity of subject and object in perpetuity rather than viewing the cleavage between them as historically contingent on alienation and reification and, therefore, as open to change in future. Kant's philosophy demonstrated the interdependence of subject and object but, by rendering the object 'in-itself' as noumenal and beyond human experience, made their separation permanent, installing capitalist alienation at the heart of modern philosophy.

Historicist philosophy since then, including Marx, has suggested that subject and object might be brought back together, based on the understanding that they were mediated primarily by labour rather than consciousness and that, while capitalist social relations held them apart in this fractured totality, they might be reconciled in a more integrated future society. Adorno discounts the latter possibility yet embraces the historicist contention, leaving readers with what Feenberg considers an untenable dilemma:

> It is impossible simply to choose between identity and non-identity, reconciliation and resistance. Regression to pre-Kantian idealism is excluded by the whole history of modern philosophy, but the bare assertion of a mysterious dissonance at the core of reality makes no sense in the post-Kantian context. How would such a dissonance enter experience? Under what concept would it be understood? How could it avoid becoming a becoming a component in the apparatus of identification, for example, an aesthetic *point d'honneur* legitimating the everyday ugliness and violence of the established order? If it fell under no concept, how would it differ from mental illness as an incoherent breakdown of meaning? The endless oscillation and mutual correction between subject and object, history and nature, recommended by Adorno is not so much a solution to the enigma as a method for cancelling any solution, most especially of course the bad ones that currently prevail in the societies of 'total administration'. (Feenberg 2005: 118)

Adorno's position turns critical theory into endless reflection on suffering caused by power's repeated attempts to impose identities, and all the twists and turns of resistance that shadow them. In contrast, Feenberg argues, Marcuse presents a compelling account of one-dimensional, dystopic society but matches this with a positive 'utopian alternative that would reconcile the non-identitarian contraries without cancelling their difference' (Feenberg 2005: 118).

Feenberg's repudiation of Adorno as regression behind Kant and his elevation of Marcuse as a visionary of reconciliation are not completely compelling, however, and the questions he asks here can be answered with reference to Adorno's work. After all, Adorno also writes of the reconciliation of subject and object but in a manner that respects their irreducible difference, writing of a constellation he calls 'Peace ... the state of distinctness without domination' (Adorno 2005: 247). For him, it is only after such a reconfiguration of subject and object has happened that 'the concept of communication, as an objective concept' might 'come into its own' (Adorno 2005: 247).

Feenberg's question about how the dissonance of non-identity enters experience is answered by Adorno's emphasis on form, which he presents as an integral moment in the experience of the artwork (e.g. 2002: 123). For him, the role of form is pre-eminent over that of meaning. In his *Aesthetic Theory*, for example, Adorno describes how, in the encounter with an artwork, 'the I becomes aware, in real terms, of the possibility of letting self-preservation fall away, though it does not actually succeed in realizing this possibility' (2002: 245) This might correspond to or even be described in terms of mental illness – the sense of an incipient, pervasive threat to one's identity is enlightening but far from joyous most of the time and might be likened to some experiences of depression. Similarly, as a defender of aesthetic modernism it might sometimes seem as if, applied to technology, Adorno could run the risk of being an apologist for austere technology designs, but this would abstract his argument from its wider dialectic, in which technology and art interpenetrate and the criteria of quality applicable to each are not reducible to the sensuous properties of either.

It seems, then, that the real point at issue in the difference Feenberg explores here between Adorno and Marcuse is not whether there can be reconciliation but rather how that state should be grasped conceptually and how the transition to it should be thought. For Feenberg it is mediated through technical politics, while Adorno restricts himself to identifying spaces in contemporary culture in which its possibility alone might be experienced. Adorno prioritises form over meaning and seems to envisage modification of the subject–object nexus happening in a way that anticipates, perhaps conditions, new possibilities of symbolic meaning. For him, experience may be more or less autonomous depending on the degree to which its formal capacities maintain a space for subjective reflection and facilitate action according to the model of peace. What separates the two views is the priority of form and meaning in their understanding of the aesthetic. Because Feenberg places meaning before form in his account of experience, he is able to construe the aesthetic in overtly political terms, while, as we have seen, Adorno is much more cautious about this.

Perhaps as a result of his rush to interpret technical designs in terms of their imputed and sometimes self-proclaimed political affiliations, Feenberg commits to some very specific aesthetic principles, which seem to me to foreclose on the actual course of contemporary design aesthetics and the role of technology in them. His attachment to modernist principles in particular is clear when he invokes Frank Lloyd Wright's architecture, for example, as a model of the integration of nature and artifice in designs that are conducive to pleasurable human experience (Feenberg 2001: 155). Feenberg writes that,

> Like the early twentieth-century avant-garde, especially the surrealists, Marcuse believed that the separation of art from daily life could be transcended through fusing reason and imagination. Marcuse thus proposes the *Aufhebung* of the split between science and art in a new technical base ...
>
> Although this program sounds wildly implausible, it makes a kind of intuitive sense. For example, we easily recognize the difference between the architecture of Mies van der Rohe and Frank Lloyd Wright. Mies shows us technology as a manifestation of untrammeled power, the technological sublime, while Wright's structures harmonize with nature and seek to integrate human beings with their environment. We will see that it is possible to save Marcuse's essential insight by developing this contrast. (2001: 155)

Designs informed by naturalistic modernism will resonate with the senses of the emancipated human creature by responding to its desire for harmony and integration.[12] These comments on aesthetics must be seen alongside Feenberg's placing of stress on the desirability of technologies that enhance human connection and facilitate communication. Feenberg perceives an alignment or affinity of strengthened communication and a reformed perception in which other people and the world are felt to be accommodating rather than hostile, or resistant and in need of control.[13]

Feenberg's confidence concerning the kinds of change aesthetic critique will demand is partly informed by the success the environmental movement has had in broadening the dominant conception of technology. The technology-ness of a thing now includes the issue of its 'sustainability', which is to say that this value has become part of what we think of and ask about when we encounter a technology for the first time – there is almost no technology use that does not now feel the pull of this question. The argument that a relatively new connotation of technology has been established here is not something that I want to take issue with,[14] but I do want to query the grounds Feenberg presents for endorsing it, because it is here that we can detect both the centrality of aesthetic critique to his theory and the fundamental ambivalence of the idea between positions that are consistent with his emphasis on contingency, relationality and difference, and others that are somewhat more focused on wholeness and reconciliation. This discrepancy becomes clearer when we look more closely at Feenberg's account of what distinguishes capitalist technology.

3 Instrumentalisation theory

As discussed previously, one of Feenberg's most important contributions to the philosophy of technology has been to introject a social and historical component into the definition of technology itself. The notion that modern, capitalist technology is different from other kinds is foundational for his project. His critical theory does not target technology's transcendental essence but only its specifically capitalist manifestation. An obvious way to approach this would be with direct reference to the historical process itself; there are numerous studies of the emergence of capitalism in terms of a series of technical and social innovations, not the least of which are those provided by Marx. However, this is not Feenberg's approach. He prefers instead to parse historical insights about modern technology through what he calls instrumentalisation theory, within which aesthetics plays a central part.

Viewed in this way, what is distinctive to modern, capitalist technology is not that it is uniquely violent or indeed that it is the source of a specifically horrible enframing of the world, but rather that it fails to compensate nature for an original violence that is present in *all* technologies. According to instrumentalisation theory, technology always has two moments, primary and secondary. These are not temporally discrete but coeval as dimensions of any present technology.

Primary instrumentalisation involves forcing nature into new shapes that comport with our wishes and entails 'a series of moments through which the object is isolated and exposed to external manipulation' (Feenberg 2001: 176).[15] At this point the influence on Feenberg of essentialist notions of violence against nature as constitutive of modern technology is particularly clear.[16] However, primary instrumentalisation is not specifically modern or capitalist and, importantly, not something Feenberg considers regrettable in itself. The difference between modern and non-modern technologies is that the latter compensated for primary instrumentalisation, which is generic, with culturally specific secondary instrumentalisations[17] that restored harmony to the world.

According to Feenberg, 'all earlier cultures are based on substantive worldviews rather than formal rational principles, which, where they exist at all, are confined to very narrow functions' (2002: 167). In those cultures, technology 'is contextualized by practices that define its place in an encompassing nontechnical action system' (2002: 177). What makes capitalist tools seem both neutral (as a formal system to be complied with) and yet more brutal is the fact that, rather than being developed to serve wider social goals that comport with cultural values, modern technology is viewed under the horizon of efficiency. Feenberg writes:

> Technology is not value neutral but rather, under capitalism the neutralization of the traditional values that governed it in earlier times adapts it to the pursuit of profit and power. These narrow capitalist values no longer respect the object, human beings or limits of any kind. (2005: 100)

In primary instrumentalisation, then, objects are decontextualised and reduced to their useful aspects. In this process human beings detach themselves from the objects so manipulated and come to assume a position of control over them. In pre-capitalist or 'traditional' societies, 'there corresponds an integrative moment' in which the objects are assigned new meanings and new symbolic status, while their users come to acquire a vocational identity in connection with them. In capitalist societies this compensatory moment is 'severely restricted' and only visible as a trace or 'remnant' (2002: 177) in medicine, or in artistic practices that use technology as raw materials.

It is this conception of the specificity of capitalist or modern technology that underscores Feenberg's belief in the necessity of an aesthetic critique, which would take the form of a demand for re-aestheticisation of the technical relation. Here there is an affinity between worker and user demands for technology that is more pleasant to use and the wider goals of progressive social change. The kind of civilisational transformation Feenberg envisages would result when such demands lead to changes that rewrite the technical code so that the horizon on technology development is broadened, altering the prevailing notion of 'efficiency' itself. The terms of such a broadening would reflect the infusion of aesthetic values associated with a recharged secondary instrumentalisation. 'An alternative modernity', Feenberg writes, 'would recover the mediating power of ethics and aesthetics' (2010: 77). It would involve a changed technical code, 'oriented towards the reintegration of the contexts and secondary qualities of both the subjects and objects of capitalist technique' (2002: 184).

In addition to his strategically construed technical politics of design, then, Feenberg envisages a 'deep democratization' (2002: 159) of technology in which it is finally 'subordinated to humanistic objectives' (2002: 165). The aesthetic critique is a crux of Feenberg's theory because it provides the bridge between these two aspects of his project. On one side, workers and others contest technology designs. On the other, each instance of success in democratising technology corresponds to a re-aestheticisation, through which progressive change touches the very meaning of technology and its articulations in the web of social relations.

The difficulty with the latter idea, however, is that it rests upon a largely unthematised presumption in favour of a harmonious relationship with nature, in which human senses are disposed to an enriched perception of the world as meaningful, while the world is made more habitable as a result of redesigned technology. This reflects an organicist bias in Feenberg's thinking, which he inherits fairly directly from Marcuse. Since technology is a potential source of disruption to the society-nature whole, the theory of secondary instrumentalisation is a normative pivot, on which critical theory of technology turns from description to prescription. The demand for re-aestheticisation is part of this, and its logic is integrative and restorative.

Feenberg's notion of a primary instrumentalisation that violates nature and which ought to be redressed through aestheticisation seems to be inconsistent with a strictly relational definition of technology. The difficulty becomes apparent when confronted with the radical empiricism of some varieties of social constructivism, including actor–network theory (ANT; Law and Hassard 2006). Bruno Latour in particular has pointed out that the idea of critique has long deployed, and to an extent been predicated on, a loaded definition of the act of making, in which the human agent is implicitly cast as coming at the world in a domineering fashion. In fact, writing in very different contexts (the sociology of religion and of art respectively) Latour and some ANT-influenced sociologists of art have suggested that 'making' need not carry any such connotation; it can involve simply letting be; it can happen even without humans being present. As Latour puts it, 'to the humble and honest work of making, they've [critical theorists] surreptitiously added a crazy hypothesis about the craftsman's domination of his oeuvre' (Latour 2013a: 142).[18]

The importance of this point lies in the discrepancy it opens up between a strictly relational definition of technology, which emphasises its constitutive entwinement in a variety of social networks, and an approach that stresses its entanglement in a dialectic of human domination and potential, in relation to inner and outer nature. If technology has no founding moment of violence that requires compensation through a second, restorative moment, then, as Latour (2013a) points out, critique loses its purchase. There is no deep violence to be compensated and no inherent human potential bound up with further development of the technological mission to overcome nature. Sharpening the relational turn in social theory, ANT prohibits postulating connections that cannot be traced through actual webs that social actors themselves recognise as connecting them and their actions to others, and which we can see tie them into other networks (Latour 2005). As Hennion writes in connection with the sociology of art, 'adding a superior, more coherent principle, whether aesthetic or social, adds nothing … it must be strictly forbidden to create links when this is not done by an identifiable intermediary' (Hennion 1995).

This line of argument threatens to cut Feenberg's theory off at the root by severing the relational definition of technology operative in technical politics from the larger project of cultural transformation. The challenge it sets for critical theory of technology is to identify a ground or source for critique that is strictly immanent to the technical relation and to technical politics. This would have to involve detaching the question of the aesthetic from its historically transcendent commitment to organicist reconciliation and repositioning it more securely in a strategic conception of the politics of technology design. In a way it is relatively straightforward to see what the call for more democracy in technology design might entail (there is an established literature to draw on regarding the kind of arrangements that might count as democratic), but the meaning of a progressive re-aestheticisation is much less clear. In my view, Feenberg's Marcusian loyalties (that is, to a dialectical reconciliation within organicist parameters) lead him into a peremptory preference for naturalist-modernist design aesthetics of the kind associated with Wright's architecture.

The 'aesthetic objection' to capitalist technology was never simply a matter of what it looked like or felt like to use. As Feenberg makes clear, it concerns the position occupied by technology in the wider culture and the global meaning of 'technology' that results from that positioning. Notwithstanding the example of environmentalism,[19] the re-aestheticisation of technology has been proceeding apace in the post-industrial era with little or no associated democratic advance. Nearly all of the digital technology that we use from day to day has a customisable interface, for example, enabling people to incorporate devices seamlessly into their lives, often transforming their embodied routines in the process. Since the late 1980s, interfaces on digital artefacts have been shaped by a design culture whose naturalist biases are largely consonant with Feenberg's approved aesthetic. The emphasis has been on creating 'environments' that support both work and play, within which the human user does not have to think about their activity in a technical way (Kirkpatrick 2004/2017).

This revolution in the way that technology is presented to its users was in some ways anticipated by Feenberg. Applying the categories of his theory to computing in the late 1980s and 1990s, he maintained a clear correlation between the then nascent tendencies towards a friendly design aesthetic and progressive social forces, contrasting them with a more technical aesthetic influenced by engineering disciplines, which he associated with hierarchies and social control:

> Systems designed for hierarchical control are congruent with rationalistic assumptions that treat the computer as an automaton intended

to command or replace workers ... Democratically designed systems must instead respond to the communicative dimension of the computer through which it facilitates the self-organisation of human communities. (Feenberg 2002: 108)

He anticipated that the result of more 'democratic' design tendencies would be 'a doubling of real social space by the virtual space of computer networks', which 'opens new communicative possibilities for everyone' (2002: 119). Feenberg's version of re-aestheticisation rests on an assumed correlation of a particular aesthetic (naturalistic modernism) with progressive social and political forces, so that he approves design principles that amplify the symbolic dimension of technology, turning computers into a 'communications medium', and condemns those that would present the computer in a more austere fashion, perhaps with command line interfaces requiring expert programming knowledge. The latter kind of design would, he argues, withhold it from mediations that involve symbolic meanings accessible to everyone.

It is clear that visually pleasing, graphical and tactile interfaces have helped groups of people to access digital technology who otherwise could not have done so. The famous architect and entrepreneurial polymath Nicholas Negroponte (1999), for example, has described how working with computers with such interfaces enabled him to overcome obstacles society places in the way of dyslexic people. This comports with widening participation in computer culture and, viewed through the lens of technical politics, is a democratic advance.

At the same time, however, user-friendly interfaces also enlarge the numbers of people who depend on digital technology as a mediating element in their cultural experience while having little or no idea how the technology works. Complex machines that are made easy to use have a manipulative aspect in which work-related imperatives can reach through symbolic communicative processes and steer people into preferred courses of action. As I have suggested elsewhere (Kirkpatrick 2015), devices that are natural to use and which pass seamlessly into users' routines have almost certainly been shaped by the very social processes invoked by Boltanski and Chiapello in their account of capitalism's recuperation strategy, which obliges workers to enjoy their work and to feel that it belongs to them.

Reflecting on the entanglement and implication of ostensibly progressive aesthetic projects and values in contemporary strategies of control leads Hal Foster to suggest that modernists should:

Beware of what you wish ... because it may come true – in perverse form. Thus, to take only the chief example, the old project to reconnect Art and Life, endorsed in different ways by Art Nouveau, the Bauhaus, and many other movements, was eventually accomplished, but according to the spectacular dictates of the culture industry, not the liberatory ambitions of the avant garde. And a primary form of this perverse reconciliation in our time is design. (Foster 2002: 19)

In sum, it is not clear that the only 'good' use of computers is communicative while more 'technical' or instrumental employments are always implicated in strategies of domination. Technical knowledge can involve difficulty but acquiring that understanding can be profoundly empowering, while 'easy' operating in sumptuous online environments makes people prey to corporate marketing and leaves them vulnerable to government and corporate spying activities.

It does not follow from this that a more austere aesthetic is preferable, only that aesthetic commitments do not fall neatly into line with political ones. Feenberg's enthusiasm for friendly computers reflects his critical perspective, in which technology's instrumental aspect and its aesthetics are divided and awaiting dialectical reconciliation, in the Marcusean scenario described above. Progressive 're-aestheticisation' is premised on the notion of a primary instrumentalisation in need of compensation, but this framing of the issue obstructs the development of a more pragmatic, context-sensitive approach to the aesthetic dimension of technical politics.

The underlying problem here is the continued hold on Feenberg's thinking of an organicist conception of society and nature. He favours naturalistic modernism because his critique of capitalist society emphasises its fragmented, disjointed character and argues that it needs repair and reintegration of its elements to become healthy. Reform proposals are assessed in light of this model of progressive change and, viewed in this way, the reconciliation of subject and object in the historical process becomes a matter of finding new forms of social life in which antagonism and domination are minimised by establishing higher levels of consistency between agents' purposes and the social whole. This approach is basically Marcusian, and as we have seen, its logic contrasts with that of Adorno's aesthetic critique.

The goal of harmonious integration is potentially tyrannical because capitalist society *is* against the individual. Adorno's dialectic was 'negative' because it asserted *both* the necessity of reconciliation *and* its radical impossibility. This is not an evasion as Feenberg alleges, but is based on acknowledgement that the subject finds no reflection of itself in the prevailing reality, apart from the fact that it seems to have been constructed to ensnare and persecute them. Attractive, user-friendly devices like smartphones can be read precisely as traps in this sense. Adorno's attention to the aesthetic as an experiential domain led him to conclude that it is only in connection with difficult artworks that human beings can find a reflection of the suffering caused by their presence-as-absence[20] in an inhuman social system. While it was conceived through reflection on so-called high arts, however, this conception of the aesthetic and its relation to political domination need not be alien to technical politics.

4 From thwarted reconciliation to superimposition

In contemporary experience the technical and the aesthetic are increasingly superimposed upon one another, and the effect is that, rather than producing a single, hegemonic truth to be overcome, possibilities multiply where users meet devices: the game is often on to establish what new technology is for, and the prevailing attitude is playful. Identity is not fixed in advance, in the sense that users co-design their artefacts by experimenting with their devices and probing their capabilities, which in turn set fresh challenges and open up new possibilities for their human users. Aesthetic experience is routinely encountered, then, as a moment in the contemporary culture of pervasive technical dabbling, and as such it is immanent to the ongoing politics of technical design.

The aesthetic, rather than being absent by design in a hegemonic, stripped-down, brutal and false neutrality and then infused with symbolic meaning by progressive forces, is always already entwined in the technical and part of its politics. Within contemporary digital technology design, the functional and the symbolic are not held apart; rather, for designers the challenge is to produce interactive software that gives access to designated functionality through mediatic elements that relate it to the purposes of the user and enable them to access it in a way that feels natural because it comports with already ingrained, habituated patterns of incorporation. This involves a politics of visibility/invisibility, concerning how much of the technical infrastructure (coded levels, etc.) the user needs to know about and what needs to be concealed to ensure they keep to the desired interactive routines. In design circles this is discussed in terms of keeping the user on track and guiding them where they want to go as seamlessly as possible.

This design practice has sociological co-ordinates in which aesthetic values map to power and strategies of control in unpredictable ways. As Maurizio Lazzaroto (2014) has pointed out, seamlessness of use is both aesthetic and ideological in contemporary capitalism, where the emphasis is on the smooth flow of consumerist experience and resolving any trace of antagonism in positive, pleasurable experiences.[21] This aesthetic effaces social agonistics and reflects the imposition of norms of conduct in ways that can bypass any need for discursive thematisation – a model of Foster's 'perverse reconciliation'. In this context, reflective critique as usually construed struggles to find anything to work with because there is an absence of discrepancies or recurrent breaks in experience that might provide it with openings.

Rather than being marked by a division of functional and symbolic that is in need of reconciliation, contemporary technological aesthetics involves this kind of superimposition. The aesthetic is not lacking or absent, and neither is it a deceitful sheen that conceals a systematic failure to integrate, or lack of contextualisation. Rather, it is implicated in strategies of misdirection based on false promises. In these circumstances Adorno's normativised aesthetic theory, with its insistence on mediated non-identity, is more relevant than ever because we are confronted not with a system of shocks[22] and jolts, reflecting the contradiction between hegemonic power and dispersed resistance, but rather with a diffuse regime whose demands are felt only in so far as subjects suffer the effects of false identification or empty performance – in other words, when they feel a sense of their homelessness in this fabricated, choreographed world.[23]

If the aesthetic is understood as a superimposition that eludes the critical metaphor of 'dominant codification' – as when we find, on reflection, that we were 'steered' towards buying an 'app' we didn't know we wanted, or that we were only able to proceed in one of two ways because a (charming) interface presented no third option – then the problem is not a lack of technical-aesthetic reconciliation. Rather, it is that the two aspects work together very well, so that authoritative demands seem natural because they cohere with our expectations and tastes to re-enforce established predispositions favoured by power.

The politics of this involve technical knowledge and the ability, or lack of it, to access, understand and operate on multiple levels, or through multiple vantage points, on the device. The struggle to feel at home, to have an authentic world-relation, is played out in efforts to master different levels that are superimposed on one another in technology design. This might be a matter of unlocking functionality that is not advertised on the front end, or of learning extra skills to get more from an app than it seems initially to offer. It might involve altering some code to modify software, but equally it could be about calibrating one's use more effectively with other software programs, network protocols or users. There is a politics of expertise and deepening understanding here that is better understood by drawing on the later Foucault's (2005) idea of an aesthetics of selfhood, a relation to oneself, than on his earlier ideas on knowledge-power.

The shaping of artefacts increasingly falls within the scope of a Foucauldian aesthetics of self-fashioning in contemporary society, and this territory is being shaped by connections that people are making for themselves in ways that are dissolving, perhaps have already dissolved, the hegemonic codification of technology as 'efficient', for example. Reflecting on the dominant, or hegemonic meaning of technology today, it's not clear that there is one: do people choose their mobile phones on grounds of efficiency? This is progress, in the sense clarified by Feenberg's theory, because it means that people are participating in contesting and shaping technology: that its representation is in question. Under these circumstances, long-established dominant meanings are perhaps more likely to be destabilised, with implications for gender norms that restrict access and use; proprietary claims over software; the right and wrong ways to use a computer network, etc. When technology itself is in question and people ask about its meaning, the rewriting of categorial orderings that, in Feenberg's terms, define a civilisation can be brought into the open and discussed as a part of the ongoing micro-sociological detail of democratic technical politics.

At the same time, refocusing aesthetic critique in this way is problematic because of the emphasis it places on individual subjects as against collective action. As others have described in detail, contemporary power works precisely by disposing people to adapt themselves to the demands of an increasingly pervasive system, rather than through the application of external, coercive force. As Dardot and Laval (2014) point out, in neoliberalism everyone is made responsible for everything that happens to them. Technology is one of the means at their disposal through which people are encouraged to respond to this situation. Given this, it will tend to dovetail with developments that fold real devices into the apparatus that Foucault figuratively described as 'technologies of the self'. This can represent an extension of domination in which aesthetic strategies of power emphasise technology's seamless, 'natural' and harmonious character, while resistance will often run in the opposite direction, disrupting this appearance. Under these conditions, critique should eschew identification with any specific set of aesthetic values and focus instead on those occasions when the meaning of technology is placed in question – any kind of question – by social actors.

The dominant idea of technology operative in such experiences corresponds not to that of a centralised hegemonic power but rather to a presence that is always also a representation, which can be placed in question and reworked with the relevant skill and acquired knowledge. In the revised account of the role of the aesthetic suggested here it remains central to technical politics. However, it is not a bridge between the proximal concerns of groups competing for control over the meanings of new technology designs and wider questions of civilisation change. The aesthetic provides no privileged point of connection with such wider shifts and does not facilitate prejudgements concerning what kind of design might be 'progressive', with reference to whether it fits more or less well in a utopia of restored wholeness. Rather, when people think about the aesthetics of a technology and how it resonates with their experience, this creates an opening to questions about its design, the desirability of their activity, what made it necessary and so on. Aesthetic experiences often lead into technical politics, and once this happens aesthetic considerations may inform the demands of oppositional movements as they set out alternative design proposals.

There is no firm basis for identifying such demands with any particular aesthetic project or movement. Rather, the kind of technology that is preferred (including its aesthetics) will be more or less 'authentic', in Adorno's sense, in so far as its design respects the non-self-identity of the technical object and maintains the openness of work (and other) spaces to intelligent determination by the person who has to operate there. This might be accomplished by creating sumptuous environments that are comfortable to occupy, but that is not likely to be straightforwardly true for all cases. Contrary to Feenberg's preference for holistic and naturalistic modernism, the aesthetic values that inform a design may be austere, deliberately challenging and kept thoroughly instrumental for perfectly good reasons other than those of domination. Designers may be concerned to subvert easy and obvious linguistic constructions on visible phenomena, for example, in the interests of encouraging users to think harder and acquire more skills. Ugliness and even brutalism may be valid aesthetic strategies: their correlation to hegemonic power is loose at best, and their consequences for technical politics unpredictable.

Notes

1 Perhaps the unifying theme of constructivism is the belief that technology designs are all fundamentally underdetermined – that is, that there is no preordained purpose that the bicycle, to use the most commonly cited example, was invented to serve. The problems technologies help to solve emerge in the course of their development and design process, rather than being clearly elaborated at the outset (Bijker *et al* 1989).

2 Hence, in *Transforming Technology* Feenberg writes that 'what defines critical theory is that it seeks out a forward-looking demand in the trace of damage that has been done to a negatively interpreted nature' (2002: 34).

3 Bruno Latour discerns a kind of condescension in critical theory, and sociology generally, when it finds meanings in situations other than those presented by actors in the situation. He urges his readers to 'resist pretending that actors have only a language while the analyst possesses the *meta*-language in which the first is embedded' (2005: 49), and goes so far as to state that 'it is never the case that the analyst knows what the actors ignore' (2005: 22).

4 The classic constructivist idea of 'closure', or 'stabilisation', rests on the idea that the disputes that shape a technology are 'forgotten' once the dominant meaning has been established (e.g. Hughes 1983: 14–15; Bijker 1997: 84–88). Feenberg's argument is more than a supplement, in that he is suggesting the form taken by closure (neutrality) is itself a product of the struggles over design, *and* that this form is the same across all, or most, cases of shaping

under capitalism. In presenting it as an instance of reification he is adopting a dialectical approach, both showing that technology is produced as inert and immutable and allowing that, as such, it acts.

5 Ian Hacking (1999) notes that this kind of unmasking has been a central part of the appeal of constructivism for critical theories.

6 Foucault is a difficult source for philosophy of technology because his denunciation of social arrangements as 'techniques' and 'instruments' is important to his polemic but nowhere substantiated as a reason to view them with suspicion.

7 Feenberg's preferred source on this point is de Certeau (1984), who builds on Foucault to distinguish between 'strategies' that constitute power and 'tactics' that mark resistance to its smooth operation.

8 Marcuse describes how in modern society, '[p]re-technological and techno-logical rationality, ontology and technology are linked by those elements of thought which adjust the rules of thought to the rules of control and domination' (1964: 138), concluding that, 'scientific-technical rationality and manipulation are welded together into new forms of social control' (1964: 146). These ideas anticipate Feenberg's own concept of 'hegemonic technological rationality'.

9 'Only a phenomenological account of values in action can make sense of the notion that aesthetics provides the normative basis for the reconstruction of technological rationality ... when Marcuse imagines aesthetics incorporated into everyday sensation as a critical force, his hypothesis implies a phenomenological conception of experience.' (Feenberg 2005: xv).

10 As when he writes of a synthesis of science and art, or the reintroduction of art into daily life.

11 Hamer (2005: 58) points out that Adorno's strategy is to use psychoanalysis to interpret the limits and threats currently posed to autonomy, and thereby to focus on human suffering. The implicit norm is of non-repressive and non-coercive subjecthood with a capacity for open-ended thought, rather than revolutionary praxis aimed at politically mediated reconciliation of self and society.

12 This is another instance of Feenberg making the move to incorporate a socio-logical element into the definition of technology but then finding that the content has changed when he goes to draw on it. Just as technology has ceased to play the authoritative role assigned to it by technocracy, so its aesthetic has already largely embraced naturalistic modernism.

13 In contrast, Adorno views communication with a degree of suspicion, contrasting it to the formal-expressive dimension of aesthetic experience, which can work precisely to undermine the reifying effects of discursive mediations.

14 Although it could be pointed out that much contemporary environmental discourse on the theme of climate change in particular takes the form of saying 'leave science to scientists', which is not consistent with the idea of a democratic, or anti-technocratic, technical politics, at least as Feenberg has presented these ideas so far.

15 In *Between Reason and Experience* Feenberg refers to this as 'de-worlding' of objects, and as 'simplifying' them prior to their inclusion in a device (2010: 72).

16 Indeed, Feenberg writes that 'primary instrumentalisation is the orientation towards reality that Heidegger identified as the technological "mode of revealing"' (2002: 175).

17 As well as aestheticisation, secondary instrumentalisation involves systematisation (artefacts make sense alongside others of their kind); vocation (people are defined through their use of the technology), and initiative (the artefact enlarges its user's scope for 'free play') (2002: 178). Instrumentalisation theory is discussed further in the next chapter.

18 Working in the Latourian vein in sociology of art, Emilie Gomart and Antoine Hennion write that action itself is sometimes best understood as 'an unanticipated gift', rather than a heroic play in the struggle of subject and object (Gomart and Hennion 1999: 222).

19 Writing about the ongoing environmental crisis, Latour points out that the earth, 'does not play either the role of inert object that could be appropriated or the role of higher arbiter' (cited by Alexandre Leskanich in his 2017 review). In other words, nature is not passive raw material, but neither is it awaiting reconciliation and integration into the historical process.

20 The basic idea here comes from Marx: human beings have to be there to operate the system but their real needs are irrelevant. The modernist artwork is isomorphic (Witkin 1998) with this, presenting people with music, to use Adorno's favourite example, that stimulates *and* defies human efforts to include it in an easy, or even pleasurable, experience of listening.

21 Discussing the role of information technology in contemporary capitalism, Lazzaroto refers to 'asignifying signs' that 'act directly on the real' (2014: 40). Asignifying semiotics depend on signifying ones but subvert them too, giving rise to experiences of sense without meaning. Diagrammatic sign machines, he says, 'shape sense'. This mirrors Adorno's emphasis on the priority of truth or form over meaning and, in the terminology of critical theory, is suggestive of a portentous reconfiguration of lived experience.

22 We should note that Adorno's use of this term is not limited to appraisal of violent or arresting images, or to the harsh conjunctions of modernist works: 'The shock aroused by important works is not employed to trigger personal, otherwise repressed emotions. Rather, this shock is the moment in which recipients forget themselves and disappear into the work; it is the moment of being shaken. The recipients lose their footing; the possibility of truth, embodied in the aesthetic image, becomes tangible. This immediacy, in the fullest sense of relation to artworks is a function of mediation, of penetrating and encompassing experience; it takes shape in the fraction of an instant, and for this the whole of consciousness is required' (Adorno 2002: 244).

23 In his study of Adorno, Witkin says that working with the materials of everyday life 'enables the artist to oppose the false reconciliation of subject and world, while preserving the subject's identity negatively through establishing a distanced and ironizing relationship between the subject and the banal forms in which its presence can be glimpsed' (Witkin 1998: 103).

5

From critique to utopia

This chapter argues that his attachment to the idea of critique inhibits Feenberg from delivering fully on the radical, utopian aims that motivate his theory of technical politics. Feenberg defines critique as a form of thought that is marked by 'persistent reference to nature, reflection and individuality', and which, on this basis, opposes 'the totalitarian power of technology'. He adds that this critique of technology, 'distinguishes critical theory from various forms of postmodernism and post-humanism' (2002: 33). At the same time, however, Feenberg accuses other thinkers in the Marxian tradition of 'trivialising or evading' the question of what the socialist technology of the future might be like, and asserts that this issue must be confronted if critical theory is 'to carry conviction' (2002: 18). He tries to develop a theory, then, that is both true to the definition of critique just cited and delivers on this promise to address the question of the nature of future technology.

As we have seen, the critical theory of technology provides conceptual resources with which to understand aspects of contemporary technology design as a negation or distortion of technology's true potential. Feenberg asserts the necessity of affirming that potential, but the critical nature of the theory means that it can only conceptualise potential negatively, as that which is not currently realised. This antinomy arises out of Feenberg's attempt to combine critique with utopian thinking, or, more precisely, to use critique to achieve utopian ends. Critique entails endless suspicion of the technical (and everything else), while utopianism requires openness to the possibility of fantastic, technologically facilitated modifications of human society and culture. Feenberg has a foot in both camps and consequently, even as he opens the door to utopian thinking, he steps back to a fairly orthodox Marxian position that restricts speculation about future technology, and imposes a check on his own insistence that critical theory must be prepared to say something positive about it, or court bad faith.

In this chapter, Section 1 returns to Feenberg's account of the 'historical essence' of technology, which is where he repudiates the notion that technology's threat (to culture, to nature) is intrinsic rather than historical. In his alternative, relational definition, technology is found in artefacts and activities distinguished by a characteristic intersection of function and meaning. Here, Feenberg identifies the technical object with the former, referring to this as the 'stripped down' version of artefacts, but emphasises that it only becomes technology proper when it is incorporated into the meaning-making practices he theorises as secondary instrumentalisation.

As we have seen, under capitalism functional objects become technology in a way that is lacking the all-important shell of reconciliation with human meaning. This accounts for the distinctively technological appearance of modern, capitalist society, while disclosing an important sense in which it is actually less technological than other cultures. The latter implication, however, is not elaborated by Feenberg and never becomes a positive principle in his theory. Instead, in the context of reflection on the meaning dimension of technology, function is presented as the truth of an object, and as such it conditions what that object can mean. Because of the negative entanglements of technology with bureaucratic and other forms of power in modern societies, function also tends to be construed negatively, especially by philosophers, as the locus of a fundamental violence done to nature.[1]

There is a version of this argument in Feenberg's theory of primary instrumentalisation. There he asserts that a basic decontextualisation of objects from their place in nature is part of the historical essence of technology. As we saw in the previous chapter, some rival theorists, especially Bruno Latour, have questioned this. In Section 2, attention turns to Peter-Paul Verbeek's post-phenomenological critique of Feenberg, in which he suggests that primary instrumentalisation might be better understood in terms of a less controversial notion of patterning, or imposing form on experience, which is then subject to cultural mediation and made meaningful. The benefit of this approach is that it allows a more active role for objects as part of the technological situation, since they participate in shaping the sense they make, so to speak, rather than always being cast as passive or violated. This idea seems to comport well with Feenberg's Marcusean search for a design practice based on harmonies rather than coercion.

However, the danger in Verbeek's position is that the notion of an ethics immanent to technology design becomes entirely relativised to a context that is understood in post-human terms. The threat here is that ethics are actually made subordinate to a techno-aesthetic principle with no discernible role for meta-level scrutiny of design choices.

Feenberg's attachment to some notion of directionality in social and historical processes serves as a counterweight to this. Section 3 discusses his use of Gilbert Simondon's idea of concretisation as a way to contain the relativism with respect to outcomes that haunts constructivism, without lapsing into Marxian technical determinism.

Section 4 suggests that Feenberg's attempt to steady the ship in this way reflects a one-sidedness in his theory, according to which the discursive and the political are always both subordinate to the technical (which carries the historical process forward through concretisation) and superordinate to it (politics redeems technology development after the fact and provides ideas that determine its meaning). The focus of technical politics is, then, the discursive mediations applied to technology rather than its substantive dimension. In his presentation of technical politics Feenberg is limited by his attachment to critique to offering a politics of technology, neglecting the utopian question of a positive technicisation of politics. He locates the operations of oppositional and dissenting agents with an interest in technology in discourse, rather than in technical practice itself. This imbalance in his theory precludes the utopian operation of advancing technical solutions to human, social and cultural problems. In this respect, his attachment to critique means that he is behind concrete developments in contemporary technical politics, where activists now develop software that changes the material realities of social and political struggle, while discourse plays a secondary role in mediating their activity.

In technical politics, as Feenberg theorises it, discourse outside technology is the source of ideas but is always obliged to follow behind technology development. This is the traditional position of critique, as negatively portrayed by Latour – it is condemned to turn up after the fact and explain why things turned out badly. In Section 5, I suggest that, in order to deliver on his utopian promise, Feenberg needs to include space for progressive substantive bias in technology design and positively identify willed technical transformation as the privileged vehicle of socialist transition. If technical politics is to be more than just a category-mistake, in which technology is judged by criteria that were developed for something else, then it also needs to include reflection on the technicisation of heretofore political questions. According to this argument, technology designs inform the value basis of the socialist model, rather than merely bearing their impress. Any vision of socialism worth its salt must include employments of technology that shape human subjectivity and rules of co-existence to create new forms of social life. Since power here operates below the level of discursivity, or deliberation on meanings, the Marxian or critical formula of democratised technology design is insufficient.

1 Historical essence

Feenberg rejects essentialist definitions of technology that construe it as inherently menacing to human values, arguing instead that technical advance is itself a human value. At the same time, he rejects the kind of determinism which maintains that culture is in the position of 'keeping up' with technical development and embracing the potential it presents. His alternative involves recognising the pervasive entwinement of technology development with questions of meaning and value, but also the ways in which that entwinement gets obscured beneath one of its effects, namely the prevailing perception of what technology is. Here reification – the abstraction of technology from the real social and historical processes that constitute it – enters the philosophical definition of technology. What makes Feenberg's theory a *critical* theory is his conviction that the task of unmasking abstraction and breaking down reification, while informed by philosophy, is also a vital moment in the creation of a different kind of technics.

He works here from within a Marxist problematic, which is concerned with the historical abstraction of human properties. Human action makes history and drives the development of human productive power, including technology. But in the course of that process, human powers become abstracted, or alienated, and appear as special properties of dominant social classes, or 'reified' entities, like the market (often credited with the rapid wealth creation of the last two and a half centuries) or technology itself (often viewed as something that acts on history from outside). Critical theory understands itself as charged with the task of dissolving these illusions to reveal the human, social processes that underlie them, and, at the same time, unmasking the operations of power that make them seem autonomous of those processes. Critique is a way of thinking that removes false appearances, and in Marx's version it is allied to emancipatory social activism and politics. Critique confirms its truth by becoming active in the situations it describes, bringing people of like mind together and empowering them not only to see through dominant illusions but also to forge new social realities grounded in co-operation that prefigure a society free from alienation and reification.

As we saw in Chapter 1, Feenberg sets himself the challenge of developing a theory that includes technology among the concerns of critique and incorporates an account of technical transformation into critical theory's ideas about agency or praxis. In this way he hopes, by way of the theory of 'democratic rationalisation', to reconstruct the idea of progress. In this version of critical theory, technology, bureaucracy and other edifices of modern society are to be taken back, as it were, by the human beings who created them and 'recoded', so that they can be set to more benign purposes.

To this end, Feenberg advances a non-reified, properly historical definition of the essence of technology, in the following terms:

> I will define the essence of technology as the *systematic* locus for the sociocultural variables that actually diversify its historical realizations. On these terms, the essence of technology is not simply those few distinguishing features shared by all types of technical practice. Those constant determinations are merely abstractions from the socially concrete stages of a process of development. It is the logic of that process which will now play the role of the essence of technology. (2001: 201)

The 'logic' Feenberg favours is the combination of two aspects of technological development that must be present in any society whatsoever, which he calls primary and secondary instrumentalisation. As we saw in Chapter 4, 'Primary instrumentalization [PI] characterises technical relations in every society, although its emphasis, range of application and significance varies greatly' (Feenberg 2001: 202). PI (sometimes referred to as functionalisation) has four elements, which Feenberg describes as 'four reifying moments of technical practice' (2001: 203):

1. Decontextualisation, in which objects are abstracted or separated from their natural contexts. Feenberg also refers to 'isolating' them and, notably, to their 'reifying extraction' (2002:179). The latter seems strange, because it means that any and all technology has a 'reifying' moment. In reification, what is true is transformed into a falsehood, and what is false is also a kind of concealed truth. Reality is present in a reified entity but in deceitful guise. It seems as if Feenberg is saying that when natural objects are abstracted in this way it involves seeing them more clearly but from a perspective that is somehow false or inauthentic.

2. Reductionism, in which objects are assessed for their promotion of affordances, or in relation to a programme of purposes. This places technology firmly within the problematics of presentation and representation. Reduction re-presents what is given in nature with a focus on useful properties, and Feenberg equates the qualities of the object that get excluded or put into the background by this process with objective 'potential' (2001: 204).

Feenberg emphasises that 1 and 2 are *objectifying* moments of PI and adds two more features of the process, which he says are moments of 'subjectivation' (2001: 208):

3. Autonomisation, which means that once isolated and related to purpose, the object confers a new freedom on the subject, namely to act in a given domain without consequences, or with protection from the feedback that such action normally triggers. This is a feature of most tools.

4. Positioning, which refers to understanding and using the laws of nature to gain strategic mastery in a given context.

The relational definition of technology locates it *at the intersection* of PI with secondary instrumentalisation (SI). In other words, there may, in principle at least, be instances of reifying practice, reduction to function, autonomisation and positioning that are not technological. Only when conjoined to SI would they be part of the process that Feenberg says constitutes technology. SI (which he sometimes refers to as 'realisation' or 'concretisation') involves:

1. Systematisation, in which objects are integrated into networks of people and other objects: long tightly linked networks in modern societies, shorter and with looser connections in traditional ones.
2. Mediation, which involves ornamentisation or decoration and the application of symbols conferring meaning: a common practice in relation to pre-modern tools, less so in the case of industrial machinery.

These are aspects of the objective life of technological artefacts, while the second two moments of SI concern their relation to human users.

3. Vocation, which refers to the emergence of a group of people who develop an affinity with the new technology in processes through which the tool 'produces' its user.
4. Initiative, which is the opening up of a margin of manoeuvre for users, in which they can experiment with uses of the technological object. This is important to the tactical dimension of technical politics.

By focusing his definition on the intersection of PI and SI, Feenberg inserts a sociological dimension into the philosophical definition of technology. Here, 'the underdetermination of technological development leaves room for social interests and values' (2001: 205). Technology emerges where it is socially shaped and 'insure[s] congruence between technology and society' (2001: 205). Feenberg describes how, in this process, technology often initially destabilises, then comes to work with and re-enforce, established social arrangements, including those based on power.

Instrumentalisation theory is a quasi-transcendental, pragmatic theory of technology as a social process. PI and SI stipulate core features of that process that Feenberg considers must be present for a thing or situation to count as technology. He elaborates on them with reference to other theories of technology. Of PI, for example, he says that its first two moments correspond to Heidegger's account of technology as 'enframing', while the third and fourth he compares to Habermas's characterisation of money and power as social steering media, which are present in most human societies. However, both of these theories famously oppose technology to the communicative, cultural dimension of human experience. Indeed, Feenberg accuses Habermas of trying to get 'a whole social critique' out of this by opposing the system to the cultural lifeworld while overlooking their embodiment 'in technical devices and disciplines that include [both and] much else besides' (2001: 203). Feenberg's own theory preserves the opposition of technical-instrumental and communicative reason, with the difference that he locates it *within* technology.

In this way Feenberg's definition introjects meta-level reflection and reflexivity into technology. Definitions, including Habermas's, that cast technology as outside of the scope of cultural, meaning-making processes are themselves a uniquely modern version of this kind of theoretical reflection. They comport with the notion of the detached expert who comes at social situations from outside, with manipulative intent and little or no regard for the human consequences of their actions. In Habermas's theory this occurs because, as part of the systems sphere, technology is ruled by an action orientation that eschews time-consuming deliberation and is thoroughly guided by technical imperatives (Habermas 1985: 202). In contrast, from Feenberg's perspective the understanding of technologists and technical action reflects the influence of reification. While Feenberg sometimes characterises technical action in similar terms to Habermas, his explanation of its character is different. In short, it is not true that technologists in modern society have no idea of what they are doing in a meta-sense – only that, having internalised these discourses, they tend not to see that having such an idea is important to what they do when they are doing it.

Feenberg interprets this situation politically and identifies it as the reification of technology in hegemonic technological rationality, which he counterposes to technical activism. He presents instrumentalisation theory as superior to other philosophical definitions of technology because they invoke ahistorical abstractions (instrumentalism, enframing) from the reality of technology, which is better understood as socially contested and thoroughly political. The introjection of these latter elements into the very meaning of technology is a welcome theoretical advance. However, in defining technology as the 'logic of a process', it is questionable whether Feenberg really proffers a definition that is less guilty of abstraction than other theories.

His analysis of technology as a process concentrates on the historically contingent and contested character of efficiency and draws out the purported play of this and associated concepts in determining the meaning of technology. By contrast, in Marx's work the 'systematic locus' of technical activity is empirical; it involves the historical interface of labour, knowledge and the productive forces. Feenberg's account, specifically in the theory of PI, includes a historically continuous, even incorrigible element of reification, which is confusing because elsewhere in the theory he emphasises that reification is a feature specific to modern, rationalised societies. If PI includes reification then modern technology involves a reified or reifying perspective on an activity that already reifies part of the world. This doubling of reification is unsettling and strikes one as symptomatic of a problem in the theory.

Feenberg's argument is that people's encounters with technology differ from their experiences with other (natural) objects because 'an initial abstraction is built into our immediate perception of technologies' (2001: 211). As we've just seen, with technical objects a 'primary function' is foregrounded and defines the interaction, and this 'seems to set us on the path towards an understanding of technology as such' (2001: 211). Even as people encounter a technical object for the first time, they experience an unusual mediation in which linguistic and aesthetic-sensory interpretative moves and accommodations are punctured or disrupted by a prior objective structure that inflects the reading of this particular class of things. The seed of reification is present in PI and cultivated by modern technology's SI, and this explains the persistent self-evidence of technology in its reified form, as authoritative, rational, efficient, etc.

In the theory of PI, Feenberg characterises this objective structure in terms that are openly derived from substantivist and essentialist philosophies. In his effort to get a sociological component into the philosophical definition of technology, he includes negative associations of technology – such as enframing, or reducing worldly interactions to instrumental purposes – while separating them from the philosophical positions that gave rise to them. His idea is that these negative characterisations have traction because they correspond to a basic level of experience or common sense, rather than as special insights of the late Heidegger. It makes sense, therefore, to recast them as historical contingencies. Feenberg makes an important contrast with traditional societies, where, he writes, 'the functional point of view ... co-exist[s] peacefully with other points of view ... none of which are essentialised' (2001: 211).

Feenberg's hermeneutics of technology, then, insists that social and cultural meanings are always integral to technology: there is no unmediated experience of technology. This point has critical import because it makes it clear that technology cannot be properly understood without acknowledging that it always combines function with some kind of meaning that makes it comprehensible to human beings, who interpret the world from a particular embodied and cultural standpoint. At the same time, the PI is intended to do justice to the fact that the element of function continues to be definitive for technology, without being its essential determinate. The narrowed definition of technology in terms of mere function, which Feenberg says predominates in capitalist modernity, is a reification because it is a socially induced distortion of technology's truth, caused by the pre-eminence of professional, technical disciplines[2] and their implication in social domination. Feenberg writes that '[a]s the prestige of these disciplines spreads, their approach to technology becomes the model for common sense and philosophy alike' (2001: 212) – that is, it is hegemonic.

Identifying technology with its function is, in Feenberg's terms, a kind of abstraction, a reification. This dimension (functionality) is not simply wrapped in signs that tell putative users what the artefact can do. It is as social-relational as any other aspect of technology: '[a]s mere physical objects abstracted from all relations, artefacts have no function and hence no properly technological character at all' (2001: 213). There is a problem for this position, however, which arises out of the argument made in the last chapter about the changed aesthetics of technology. The character of the technical inflection, or the way in which the technical object intrudes (obtrudes) on sense- or meaning-making activities seems to have shifted even in the years since Feenberg first made this accommodation with his substantivist precursors in the philosophy of technology. In particular, the notion that when encountering a technical object one is guided or steered by a *reified* function, and that this defines the interaction as coldly instrumental or spiritually empty, jars with the experience that most people have of contemporary, especially digital, technologies. In other words, it is no longer common sense. The relationship people have with their smartphones, activity trackers or other digital gadgets of everyday life does not match the description this seems to imply of them, as reified and authoritative.

2 Hermeneutics and the object

Post-phenomenology considers Feenberg 'humanist' because he only treats of technology as it is constructed or discursively mediated. Peter-Paul Verbeek, for example, agrees with Feenberg that there is no transcendental meaning of technology (instrumental efficiency gains, narrowed worldview, etc.) that underpins (or overrides) socially constructed ones (Verbeek 2013). He proposes to approach technology at the level of individual artefacts rather than viewing them all as the expression of a way of thinking or as occupying a particular predetermined place in our social imaginary (Verbeek 2006: 196). Technologies are as they manifest in context and not instances of a universal class sharing common properties, or dependent social variables subject to the rule of their human designers. They are entwined with other situated elements and agentic, so that the question of their identity is dynamic and open, as it is for all social actors. Technologies are always both emergent in this sense and irreducible to other levels of description, including the idioms of explanatory physical science that might be expected to account for their behaviour in advance.

While Feenberg's instrumentalisation theory is not essentialist, or even substantivist in the accepted sense of that term, it does stipulate, in a pragmatic invocation of the idea of function, what historical technical artefacts *are* – what makes them all technology. This definitional move is refused by Verbeek. Instead, he proposes that technology has the constant feature that it 'gives form to human existence' (2006: 48) and 'imposes form' on our experience of the world (2006: 209). In this sense, it plays a role in shaping human existence but one that operates outside of linguistic mediation and symbolic meaning. Crucially, moreover, the form it confers is not specifiable in advance or deducible from essentialist premises or historical constants, including reification. From this perspective, all of the moments in Feenberg's instrumentalisation theory are only contingencies, features of a historically specific experience of technology. Technology produces a 'pattern' (2006: 180) in human existence, but which pattern it produces varies between instances.

Like Feenberg, Verbeek postulates two layers to the technical artefact – one embodied, shaping form and conferring pattern, the other involving symbolic appearance, meanings and discourse. For him, each artefactual encounter involves the becoming of things and people, shaping a world that appears a certain way to humans. Verbeek's thesis is post-phenomenological because of the active role he assigns to objects as agents in the process of their own production: they exist in a sense that goes beyond (and conditions) their appearance to and meaning for human beings. He calls for a design culture that anticipates the moral consequences of artefacts' agency, as part of the process of their production. Rather than deferring normative or moral questions to the abstract consideration of their likely impact on social contexts, he regards norms as immanent to the design process, and assigns ethical weight to the artefacts themselves as part of this. For this reason, Verbeek writes of the intrinsic desirability of transparent designs (2006: 228) that would enable users to see the full workings of a given device, rather than more simplified interfaces tailored to meet requirements anticipated by designers, which then become prescriptive and limit in advance what artefacts may say or do.

This sounds similar to technical politics, in that Verbeek places ethics as internal to the technology design process, but, unlike Feenberg, he does not understand this in terms of opposed instrumentalisations (PI/ SI).[3] For Verbeek, Feenberg's technical politics is restrictively humanist because, although he locates democratic potential within technology's developmental trajectory, he identifies the source of progressive ideas as outside of it in the realm of public political discourse.[4] Describing the historical process in which technology has been shaped by capitalism, Feenberg observes that the exclusion of values from the technical sphere sees them resurface outside it, so that '[t]he very same process in which capitalists and technocrats were freed to make technical decisions without regard for the needs of workers and communities generated a wealth of new "values," ethical demands forced to seek voice discursively' (2002: 22). Technical politics, then, involves the importation of these discursively formulated values into the technical sphere as currently constituted. It is in light of this that Feenberg argues that one of the goals of the critical theory of technology is 'to account for the increasing weight of public actors in technological development' (2002: 24).

Elsewhere, when he discusses the example of changes to computing in the 1980s, Feenberg describes matters differently. There he identifies progressive elements within the technical professions as Foucauldian 'specific intellectuals' (2002: 100). Efforts to make computers into communication tools rather than sources of top-down management control, he says, were brought about by 'specific intellectuals act[ing] in the margin of maneuver associated with a technical domain in order to transform the code establishing that domain' (2002: 101). The two accounts are not contradictory, and in practice Feenberg wants us to believe that both things are true: non-technical publics lobby for change and progressive members of technical professions can act with similar values in mind, or even be influenced by putative users.

The ambiguity over whether this occurs from the outside, as action upon the code to change it, or as a mutation from within the code itself matters, though, because it suggests a one-sidedness in the critical theory that is not present in Verbeek's argument. Technical politics is concerned with values formulated outside of the technical sphere – communication, education, democracy, the aesthetics of usability and so on – and the progressive nature of some intra-technical action is identified as such only in so far as it appears to comport with those values. Yet this neglects what is specifically *technological* about technology, and what it might do to enhance politics and alter prevailing social and cultural values. Instead, we are told that 'everywhere technology goes, centralised hierarchical social structures follow' (2002: 24), which preordains the failure of technical politics. Feenberg writes as if the technological aspect of technology, which in the dystopian technological imaginary has always been on the side of power, can take care of itself and needs no protection or advocacy from philosophy. For Verbeek, in contrast, design is not the domain of codes that provide openings for extraneous norms, because norms are already immanent to it and the ethical character of technology development is not an 'after the fact' assessment controlled by the (mournful) wisdom of hindsight.

Consequently, Verbeek points out, 'it is precisely the failure to recognise that things have a moral valence that gives rise to technocracy' (2006: 216). This point is very close to Feenberg's suggestion that capitalist formal bias involves not a socially induced distortion of the technical object so much as a failure to control or contain it in a SI. But comparing the two views reveals the limits set by Feenberg's attachment to critique. Verbeek's point is that there seems to be no reason in principle why a failure of SI, of the kind that is central to Feenberg's diagnosis of modernity, might not result in spectacularly benign or beautiful devices unencumbered by the impress of extraneous political or ethical valuations. The difference here is subtle but important because Feenberg's quasi-transcendental characterisation, while cautiously formulated, appear to be basically concerned to combat a technology historically associated with power, rather than to positively affirm its capacity to substantively alter social reality.

Instrumentalisation theory draws too much on a hermeneutics of suspicion applied to technology to be able to facilitate the conceptual pivoting that Feenberg requires from his theory. To move from critique of technology to utopian projection concerning its role in a more benign future, its ambivalence needs to be cancelled and its transformative power affirmed. The idea of function is less useful here than the notion of form, invoked by Verbeek in the comments just cited. The abstraction and isolation of technical elements described in instrumentalisation theory can be retained, but describing these as drawing out function already presupposes an understanding of the way that technology is integrated with social purposes – in other words, it strays into describing the capitalist SI.[5] In contrast, the idea of PI as the imposition of form that conditions meaning helps to clarify the idea of a 'systematic locus' that defines the historical essence of technology.

However, a problem remains with Verbeek's position, namely that it involves a post-modern relativism about values in technology that Feenberg rightly wants to avoid. While he feigns to disavow such relativism, Verbeek acknowledges that his theory is 'motivated by the post-modern aversion to context-independent truths' (2006: 115). If all the relevant values and norms are immanent to the technology situation and, importantly, there is no way to specify what technology ought to be for that is not some kind of 'humanist' imposition, then it seems that anything might go. Feenberg attempts to reconstruct the notion of technological progress in order to establish and clarify a sense of the overall direction or purpose against which technology development ought to be assessed.

3 Concretisation, subjectivation and the technological monad

When Feenberg defines technology in terms of its social logic, he invokes a specific entwinement of the dimensions of function and meaning, which he clarifies with reference to Gilbert Simondon's idea of concretisation. In this concept notions of form and function are, helpfully, combined. Simondon distinguishes 'technicity' in artefacts from their usefulness, arguing that it is characteristic of technical systems that their structures felicitously incorporate uses and relations to the environment, in a process of 'elegant condensation' based on 'the discovery of synergies between the functions technologies serve and between technologies and their environments' (Feenberg 2001: 217).

Feenberg takes over this account of technology's tendency to expand and to incorporate new purposes as it unfolds, and argues that its logic is progressive. He writes that '[t]he process of concretisation has a progressive character: design can be ordered in a sequence going from the most abstract to the most concrete' (2001: 217). Since new knowledge is manifest in new technical structures, technology development combines cognitive advance with social and cultural development. Finding purposes that technology can fulfil is part of a 'reflexive accommodation' to the new capacities that technology presents as it differentiates itself. This progressive movement includes enhanced economic efficiency but, potentially at least, other things as well.

Feenberg attempts to adapt Simondon's perspective by opening it up to constructivism, arguing that 'functions', in Simondon's sense, 'gather social groups' (2001: 218), and in this way technology forms a 'systematic locus for the sociocultural variables that ... diversify its historical realizations' (2001: 218). However, this marriage of Simondon and constructivism is, at best, problematic. Constructivism's social processes select from technological properties that are inherently contingent, even haphazard, in their development, because they are technically underdetermined. Moreover, and especially in Feenberg's version, these processes involve social struggle and antagonism, and their outcomes are strongly contingent on how those political contests are resolved. In contrast, Simondon's theory of concretisation follows a very different logic, which he likens to the process of crystal formation out of a chemical milieu. There is a clear discrepancy between the proposition that technological designs tend to acquire functions as they unfold in accordance with such a strong sense of pattern and the argument that they are shaped by social and political struggles.

Feenberg acknowledges that constructivism is 'obviously incompatible with Simondon's tendency to determinism' (in de Vries 2015: 3), but tries to create a synthesis based on 'ambiguities' in Simondon's presentation of his theory. He recognises the scale of the challenge, acknowledging that while constructivism excludes any idea of abstract or autonomous technicity, Simondon's theory appears to allow no role for social shaping in the genesis of technologies. Feenberg's synthesis involves assimilating formal technicity to generalities of social theory, especially the idea of rationalisation. He writes that 'ever since Marx and Weber, the mainstream social critique of modernity has emphasised technification, the cultural generalisation of what can loosely be called technicity' (de Vries 2015: 3), a move that aligns Simondon's concept to the idea of societal rationalisation. It is difficult not to consider this rather forced, however. There is, it seems to me, an affinity between the idea of technicity and Verbeek's notion of form, but it is tendentious to attempt to align these ideas with anything like societal rationalisation.

In Feenberg's hands, then, Simondon's concept of concretisation is primarily normative – that is, it describes the logic of technology development as it ought to be (2001: 219–220), if its potential were not thwarted by modern society. Simondon rejects the application of 'external' criteria of quality, including profit and utility, to technical artefacts. The idea of concretisation emphasises that the becoming of technologies involves movement from abstraction in design towards what he calls the 'superabundance' of acquired functions, in excess of anything that might have been anticipated at the outset:

> Concretisation brings not only new properties, but complementary functions, beyond those sought after, which we might call 'superabundant functions'. ... These properties of the object surpass expectations; it is a partial truth to say that an invention's purpose is to attain an objective, to produce an entirely predictable effect. An invention is brought into being in response to a problem, but its effects extend beyond the resolution of the problem, due to the superabundant efficacy of the created object when it is a true invention. (Cited in Chabot 2013:15)

Simondon's concept has utopian implications, since it implies a progressive logic of technology development involving the open-ended accrual of functions to technical elements. This logic combines social and technical factors, and it suggests a polyvalent, rather than ambivalent, account of technology's relationship to social change. Simondon does not sharpen the opposition of concretisation to capitalist distortion in the way that Feenberg does – he describes how particular points in capitalist mining operations become lively centres of innovation (Chabot 2013: 13), for example, rather than decrying capitalism's distorting effects.

Feenberg identifies concretisation as setting out a 'path to wider inclusion through redesign' (2017: 181), and his proposal is to use this concept to outline a suitably 'complex trajectory of progress' (2001: 218). But the alliance with Simondon is not without its challenges. For example, a

discrepancy is apparent when Feenberg writes of 'strategies of concretisation', which aligns it not with tactics and the perspective of grass roots
technology activists but rather with the 'positioning' moment of PI, in
which technology is articulated to the interests of power working through
a depleted SI. The fact that societal rationalisation (or differentiation),
stripping down, and so on, run into the future, while, on his reading,
concretisation repeatedly brings value questions back in, leads Feenberg
to call concretisation the 'technological unconscious' (2001: 220) of modernity. At this point, concretisation becomes the intuitive foundation of
critique; a reminder of harmony and integration as lost features of our
relation with the natural world, rather than a method of utopian future-
projection. The 'technological unconscious' pulls us back to the truth of
a more integrated technological trajectory but, as such, it is a kind of
repressed memory that surfaces in the wake of technical advance, to call
for the reassertion of imperilled human values.

As we have seen, Feenberg refers to neglected potential in modern
technology caused by its shaping by capitalist purposes. He argues
that an alternative civilisation might recover what he calls 'traditional
technical values' (especially vocation and self-realisation through tool
use), or it could produce its own version of SI, invoking new values and
strengthening concretisation. In this way, technical politics combines
the 'themes of substantivist critique' with opposition to capitalism.[6]
Simondon's theory can help with this if it is articulated to more future-
facing parts of Feenberg's theory.

One of the challenges faced by critical theory of technology is the
absence of a thoroughly immanent standard of evaluation for technical
design practice – a standard of the kind that Verbeek seems to be after.
Feenberg's attempt to grasp the 'historical essence' of technology provides
resources with which to think that issue through, not least because it was
developed in part to counter post-modern and relativist arguments. The
difficulty is that if technology is only as constructed, or as it emerges in
the technological situation as described by post-phenomenology, then
there is no way to place its development in relation to wider questions
of social advance or progress.[7] Verbeek's immanent ethic of the technological object is, in this sense, insufficiently robust because it doesn't
facilitate the evaluation of technologies against the wider backdrop of
questions of civilisational value or historical directionality. Simondon's
ideas of technicity and concretisation can help with this, since they present an idea of the relational essence of technology (its form, as against
the more sociological 'function') and a theory of the logic of its unfettered
development, which is both aesthetic and normative.

These ideas might facilitate an alternative theorisation that
accounts for the way in which changes at the level of ontology (alterations to capabilities and affordance in the world) are stitched into

ontic meaning-making processes wherein people gain familiarity with techniques and operate with them from day to day. As we saw in the last chapter, this is the goal that Feenberg sets for theory in his idea of a re-aestheticisation of technology. The underlying difficulty is to reconcile the fact that some descriptions of technology seem to grasp its more fundamental aspects with the equally true proposition that 'an adequate definition of real technology, as opposed to the narrow, idealised cross-section studied by engineering involves much besides the formal-rational properties of devices' (2001: 216). That is, there can be social disputes and contests over design in which critical theory can take an interest, but some perspectives on the technical object yield more truth about it than others – which is problematic because these are the ones most likely to be monopolised by expert groups aligned with power. Feenberg's suggestion is that technology's truth can be a distinctive marriage of formal function and human interests, of the kind we find in medicine and sedimented in the vocational practice of doctors, engineers and others who are technologists, and who faithfully create themselves as subjects through the technical encounter that defines them and their tools. Feenberg's notion of a technical subjectivation provides the framework within which to think this technical-political relation.

The theory of SI places technology in the problematic of representation central to Adorno's conception of critical theory. Adorno's version of critique seeks to loosen the hold of established epistemic models by showing that each identity has a 'natural history' (Hullot-Kentor 2006) involving an excess that is both essential and excluded. One of the aims of this approach is that of allowing objects to speak, which is achieved by highlighting the resistances concealed within any act of naming. This can be illustrated with reference to cultural practices like music, which, at its most 'stripped down', is just noise that can be heard by humans but which becomes something more than that when its bare mechanism is incorporated into culture. Experiences of the new within music (or art generally, and perhaps also technology) raise the question of what is included in the definition, and by emphasising this as a point of methodological principle, Adornian analysis generates glimpses of music as such as it passes between moments of relative fixity and those in which the raw material escapes the nomological net. Moments like that of the captivating movement of a mechanism detached from any function or purpose are indicative of how this argument, developed in connection with art, might apply to technology.[8]

Adorno writes of a 'shudder'[9] produced by some artworks, when the subject temporarily loses the conviction of self-identity and is open to the truth of its ontological precarity. The pervasive uncertainty concerning what counts as real on either side of this encounter gives rise to a subjective sense of one's self as merely a passing and barely distinct representation: 'The I is seized by the unmetaphorical semblance-seeking consciousness that it itself is not ultimate but semblance' (2002: 246). Now, the shudder is a moment in the mediation of form as the objective within the subject. Adorno compares the role of critique here to that of psychoanalysis in relation to dreams or other psychological symptoms (2002: 137). Only critique is able to distinguish the presence of form, which serves as a kind of curative insight, much as psychoanalysis helps a neurotic to identify the real source of their suffering and thereby liberates them from intrusive or compulsive thoughts. Critique leads the subject to move with the resistant or oppositional content of the artwork itself as it refuses the dominant ordering of reality. Critique here creates a back channel between the inner content of artworks (their form) and the unconstrained freedom of thought that would be an emancipated subject – Adorno refers to 'logic without conclusion' (2002: 137) – that is implied in the critically mediated encounter with authentic artworks.

In artistic subjectivation the experience of form implies a change of constellation, a new reality in which subject and object are reconfigured and towards which true or authentic thought is inclined. Adorno's theory is Marxist in the sense that it retains belief in both a form of subjectivity worthy of a better life and a historical truth adequate to it. In aesthetic experience they are both contained within what he calls the 'aesthetic monad' (2002:123) to indicate how this relation is abstracted from social and historical reality, mirroring it in a way that resists and repudiates it. In the changed techno-social configuration that is digital culture, it makes sense to adapt this line of thought to develop Feenberg's notion of a technological subjectivation. The role of critique is to bring the technological unconscious to consciousness in connection with specific concretisations. Its truth, like that of art, is the promise of a better world that cannot be represented directly. Faithful to this, the technologist's action is always a procedure that both explores (differentiates) and concretises. Fidelity to technological truths becomes, then, the effort to delineate a new world within the old.

Technological subjectivation differs from that of art, however, in that rather than opening a back channel to history it almost invariably involves a play for future significance.[10] Rather than rejecting technical reason as intrinsically instrumental and in need of compensation or correction, it should be understood as necessitating precisely the kind of openness to the object that is invoked in Adorno's theory. Invention is a process that involves an intuition of the ways in which materials behave; whether this involves an appreciation of mechanism and movement or of the intrinsic elegance of lines and blocks of code, all true invention has an aesthetic dimension. Technical subjectivation involves the kind of profound questioning that Adorno associates with the aesthetic, in which one's own identity is at stake. This much seems to be entailed in

Feenberg's reference to technology as a subjectivation: through it, individuals become something substantively different than they were before. An encounter with the technological event and the decision to embrace a particular meaning subjectivates its human participants at the same time as it allows objects to say something new. It is also, of necessity, a political development because it simultaneously involves a wider claim to relevance, as a vision of future society. Whenever a technological subjectivation occurs it implies an (often very radical) agenda for social change.

Feenberg's version of this process involves vocation: a calling to work in an area that is often the basis of specialisation and expertise. There is a strong resonance between this calling to and love of technology and Adorno's analysis of the transformative potential of the artwork. A subject of technology is one who knows its potential from the inside, so to speak: who embodies the mesh of technical and human in its experimental phase. Their being rests on a decision or decisions about new technical capabilities, which they select and attach themselves to. This is a two-way process in which the loosening of prior subjective identifications[11] creates a space in which objects can speak and act.

There is a connection here with Verbeek's thesis that the technological artefact is an ethical agent in excess of the descriptions applied to it by technologists. The latter's post-modernism amounts to the idea that adopting an inclusive approach to artefacts as agents can be understood as ethical practice, without postulating any connection to wider narratives, in particular to any idea of progress. This is unsatisfactory because normative claims of the kind that are important to technical politics must submit themselves to the judgement of the historical process as movement towards greater human self-realisation. The cultural condition of post-modernity highlights the lack of any political bridge from localised concern with ethics in design to history as arbiter in this sense, since there are apparently no historical narratives within which the ethics of increased sensitivity to objects acquires socio-historical significance. Here, Simondon's idea of concretisation provides a starting point, since it entails a reconfiguration of subject and object that will be an enhancement of both.

4 The reification of critique

The idea of technical politics was to some extent conceived in response to a situation in which increasing numbers of people started to demand an active role for themselves in technical decisions that affected their lives or concerned them. As seen above, Feenberg emphasises that the interventionist consciousness required for technical politics is an extra-technical mediation. He argues that those who are excluded from decision-making 'have recourse to discourse' (2002: 153), where they can discuss technology and formulate their own demands. However, if technicisation is stripped of its associations with the negative formulations in the theory of PI, then the question of the technicisation of politics and culture is a positive, potentially optimistic one. The fact that Feenberg never asks it is the legacy of a *critical* theory that thinks of itself as the locus of a special kind of rationality that is opposed to instrumental reason. Attachment to this figure of thought prevents Feenberg from fulfilling one of his own strictures on what a critical theory must do. Critique prevents us from thinking through the transformation of technology, technical infrastructure and technical practices as part of the transition to a new civilisation, and from thinking technically about that transition.

Epistemically, critique first defined itself as defence of a *non-technical* way of understanding the world.[12] Its fundamental task is to distinguish dimensions of human culture that should not be subject to scientific analysis and routinised through the application of technical 'solutions'. Feenberg's attachment to critique is therefore in tension with his goal of progressive rationalisation implemented through democratised technology design. In his theory, even though technology and rationalisation are now held to be open to alternative configurations, it seems that they are still to be comprehended from within a framework that is inherently suspicious of them. But if alternative, democratic or subversive rationalisations are possible then there is reason to expect that technical designs inspired by them might be compatible with, for example, family meals and the management of interpersonal relationships.[13]

A basic principle of technical politics is Feenberg's argument that ethics applies to technology design. This leads him to approve of some tendencies within technology design over others, so that he writes, for example, that 'any technology that enhances human contact has democratic potentialities' (2002: 91). However, the normative foundations for this judgement are never clarified, and this creates the impression that they are not immanent principles but seem to be brought to the technology situation from outside. The obvious source for Feenberg's choice of communication as the core value is Habermas, who identifies agreement and consensus as conditions of possibility of linguistic communication and, for that reason, serviceable as the basis for an immanent ethic of non-systematised social situations. However, Feenberg rejects Habermas's opposition of communication to the systems sphere, because it makes technology amoral and places it beyond the reach of democratic control. If he is unable to endorse communicative ethics because it excludes technology and technical action in principle, it is difficult to see how Feenberg reaches his own prescription for good technology design as intrinsically favouring communication. The question begged by this move is whether a technology might be deleterious to human connect-edness, perhaps fostering more privacy or enabling people to avoid one another, yet still be *good technology*.

Here, as elsewhere, Feenberg endorses the sentiments but not the thinking behind an essentialist criticism of technology and its erosion of culture. The problem is that these sentiments are not in themselves uncontroversial and, separated from the arguments that gave rise to them, they appear as personal preferences. Politically, critique conceives itself as involved in the defence of democratic politics, as the domain of free, undistorted communication against the incursions of 'the system' (including technology). Feenberg's attachment to this opposition, not-withstanding his attempt to install it internally to technology, prevents him from developing a theory of willed technological transformation, which is a necessary point of departure for utopian thought.

The theory of technical politics opens up technology and technical reason to discussions about values and politically motivated transform-ations, but, as we have seen, the model for reform is always a matter of impressing values onto technology; it never concerns the technical trans-formation of social or political practices and values. Defining the core of technology in terms of PI, Feenberg locates interventions and struggles over meaning only at the level of SI, where technological forms are socially mediated. In other words, what is at stake in technical politics is the meaning of technology, rather than its form or what it does in a sub-stantive, physical or material sense.[14]

In consequence, technical politics as Feenberg conceives it involves an imposition of politics (its values, ends and rationality) onto technology. But if it is not to be based on a category-mistake, in which technology is simply judged by criteria that were really developed for something else, then technical politics also needs to include space for the technicisation of heretofore political questions. The idea of technical politics needs to be rebalanced to reflect the fact that, as Verbeek points out, technolo-gies bring their own arguments to bear upon issues of normative import. In a fully developed dialectic of technical politics, technology should be part of politics; and technical values, once they are drawn out through liberated technical practice, should be inscribed in political solutions and cultural innovations.

Activists are already creating technologies that propound alternative values as a matter of their substance rather than shaping technology in line with ideals and values (like communication) derived from discourse. An example of this is the 'Universal Automation' browser extension software created by hackers in the UK in 2013, in response to the government's 'Universal Jobmatch' programme.[15] Universal Jobmatch was a job search website for unemployed workers which enabled the Department for Work and Pensions to monitor benefit claimants' job-seeking activities. People who failed to apply for enough jobs would be subject to reductions in benefit, or 'sanctions'. Under the slogan 'Workers of the world ... Relax!', Universal Automation software automated the job application process, enabling benefit claimants to circumvent the regime by applying for hundreds of jobs in a few seconds.[16]

In Feenberg's terms, the Universal Automation program is an example of progressive substantive bias (a category he rejects – see Chapter 2 above), since it has no other use than supporting unemployed workers in their struggle to live free from state harassment. The concept of technical politics needs to be rebalanced to reflect this kind of development in which, just as technology is opened up to receive values, *social and political goals are formulated and implemented in and through technical action*. Although it is only a piece of software, Universal Automation is a more articulate statement of the right to social security than any number of blog posts, magazine articles or books of critical theory. To comprehend and move with this kind of development, critique needs to shed its own self-identity, its image of itself as something that is not technical. When critique stops reifying itself it will be able to identify positively with thought that is active in the world, and attach itself to objects that actively shape the future.

5 Technologically authorised socialism

As we have seen, through his idea of the technical code Feenberg has demonstrated that technology is open to multiple articulations and identified this as an opportunity for progressive politics. In this sense, his work marks an important advance over previous Marxian scholarship, when he writes that:

> Scientific-technical rationality is not an ahistorical monolith that must be defended or rejected as a whole but an evolving complex of attributes that can be configured in a variety of ways with diverse social implications. Alternative rationalisations depend on which among these attributes is emphasised. (2002: 131)

Technical politics is the field of struggle opened up by this insight. The competing social agents described by constructivism, who seek to impress different meanings onto artefacts in the development process, are now understood as the bearers of values related to political perspectives. Successful 'rationalisations' alter the significance of technology and its place in society and, potentially at least, correspond to a wider process of democratisation. Feenberg draws technology into politics and makes it possible to envisage a different kind of technological civilisation.

The ultimate aim of technical politics is to trigger a global transformation affecting what technology means. Feenberg writes of a series of 'mutually supporting transformations' (2002: 27), leading to a superior civilisational model. His vision of technical politics can be represented as a series of oppositions:

Technical rationality	Communication
Hierarchy	Democracy
Brutalist aesthetic	Naturalist aesthetic
Managerial control	Social connection
Neutrality	Ethics

Capitalist modernity favours the tendencies in the first list but leaves a series of openings through which people can push for items in the second. Ultimately, this kind of grass roots activity will tip the whole meaning of technology over into something compatible with human self-realisation and not subordinate to the demands of the capitalist social system.

Feenberg argues that technology should subserve the societal goal of widening democracy, and that enhanced democratic control over technology design is the way to achieve this. His model of socialist transition retains Marx's emphasis on the contradiction that capitalism engenders between the need for skilled, knowledgeable workers to operate sophisticated machinery on one side and the requirement that they serve as docile, unquestioning subordinates on the other. As workers become more educated, so they are more likely to perceive the iniquities and inefficiencies of capitalism and to use their expertise to change the situation (1991: 30). Feenberg argues that this contradiction is manifest today and is part of the explanation for the growing interest in technology design. Even if, most of the time, squabbles over the meaning of a technology are mundane reflections of sectional interests with no obvious bearing on larger questions, it remains the case that a great deal 'is decided ... by the shape of our tools' (2002: 19). Feenberg maintains that 'the very definition of modern life is up for grabs' (2002: 120) in disputes over technology design.

Verbeek's post-modernist version of technical politics maintains that we can benefit from the critique of this or that individual technology – indeed, that such critique is part of what technology design involves – but that there is no wider historical eschatology that helps to orient these decisions. This is unsatisfactory because it relativises the ethical dimension of technology design and defers the larger questions persistently raised by technology development. We can summarise this by saying that Verbeek wants to let objects speak but has no deep interest in what they have to say. Embracing concretisation as a utopian moment involves working with the open-ended advance of technological form as it meshes with the human material of history. Within this, techno-logical events are not straightforwardly deterministic but are mediated through subjectivations founded on human decisions, and utopian pol-itics affirms those decisions when they are guided by the conscious belief that a better future is possible – that is, they correspond to the immanent ethics of technology design.

Feenberg rightly challenges those who seek a quicker, more direct route to a superior civilisation to explain how such a transition will be possible without social action aimed at challenging the technical division of labour – that is, the deep entanglement of technology with expertise and hierarchy-reproducing knowledge practices. However, the one-sided nature of his theory reveals itself here: Feenberg's assumption is that the goal is *democratic* technology, whereas from the standpoint of techno-logical subjectivation a superior civilisation primarily requires *better* technology. This is a matter not so much of bringing technology under political control as of allowing technologies political speaking rights. Just as art establishes an inner connection between a non-identical subject and a more authentic future, so technology too can inspire the convic-tion that a new world is possible: indeed, this is the benign promise of all technology before it gets thoroughly entangled with capitalist and other societal logics. More than that, it can begin to implement that conviction as part of a pre-configurative utopian strategy.

Rather than bearing the impress of particular, contingent values, better technology would have implications for the meaning of those values in practice, including democracy. What that technology consists in, its fun-damental orientation, can itself be a focus for political will-formation. Technology design can be politicised by raising value questions within its design, and, as Feenberg points out, there is evidence that changes like this have already happened to design culture. However, seeking better technology as part of a superior society is not only a matter of imagining a world where workers can determine what technology is from day to day (the grass roots conception of technical-political freedom); it also involves imagining a world in which technology acts on people to produce new dispositions, habits of mind – in short, different kinds of sociality.

I submit that a rebalanced technical politics should take seriously the polyvalent, multi-dimensional, immanent logic of technology itself and incorporate the possibilities it presents into theoretical reflection on the future. This properly expands on the utopian moment implicit in the notion of new concretisations, by establishing conceptual space for a willed transformation of technical infrastructure. It involves acknow-ledging technological subjectivation as a moment in technical prac-tice that is fundamentally autonomous of political considerations but invariably consequential for society and politics. Thinking this through requires that we accept the technicisation of politics as the dialectical corollary of the politicisation of technology.

As the later Foucault showed, the modern subject is a product of structured predispositions that are often technically implanted. Other experiential forms of subjectivity will be selected and foregrounded by different technical apparatus in the future. In recent decades the internalisation of work discipline and performative norms by a 'streamlined subject' have been facilitated by technologies that produce individuals who justify themselves and their actions in terms of efficiency and rational self-interest, not because they have deliberated or reflected on these values but because they were sedimented in the socio-technical environment. For the most part, social media notwithstanding, civic responsibilities have not been part of this reprogramming of the self.

In the age of social media it is anachronistic to pretend that questions of privacy, meaning, the nature of love and so on may not be susceptible to technical 'solutions'. A rebalanced technical politics could focus on substantive alterations to existing social media technologies, with the goal of inclining human behaviour in specific, desired directions. The values of any new society will be played out in a change of fundamental attitudes on the part of citizens, and there is no reason to expect them to do this on their own. Instead, new concretisations of subject and object can be envisaged that incline people to be socially responsible citizens, that promote and support acts of solidarity and kindness, personal traits of courtesy, good manners and tact. Social credit systems which track peoples' behaviour and reward them for good conduct, stimulating a more co-operative disposition, have alarmed some left-liberal commentators (Greenfield 2018), but working with the form of technology to bring about substantive social change almost certainly means being prepared to countenance similar projects, in which technology changes the meaning of ideas like freedom and democracy.

Notes

1 This is what leads Feenberg's critics to discern an ambivalence in his work on the issue of essentialism – see earlier discussions. In this chapter I am suggesting that the real issue is his attachment to critique.

2 These disciplines embody a refined understanding of function, detached from considerations of meaning; hence, in the terms mooted above they contain truth but in a false perspective.

3 Similarly, Douglas Kellner argues that since aesthetics and function are 'equiprimordial', there is no reason for Feenberg to hypostatise their separation, or to refer to the resulting theory as 'instrumentalisation' theory (Arnold and Michel 2017: 278).

4 It is worth noting that this is the condition of application for Feenberg's own work, or of its link to praxis. Critical theory, it seems, cannot be parsed into technical manuals or engineering textbooks.

5 As when Feenberg writes that 'The concept of function strips technology bare of values and social contexts, focusing engineers and managers on just what they need to know to do their job' (2001: 213).

6 Feenberg writes that this is the 'heady air we must breathe if we want to make a fundamental difference to the shape of technical advance' (2001: 224).

7 Indeed, there seems to be no non-culture-specific way to identify it as technology.

8 An illustration of this idea of form which can pass between functional settings, acquiring different meanings when it gets re-embedded in a new context of use, is provided by mechanical alphabets created in the century before the development of industry in Europe. These proto-machines were wooden models, whose 'functions' are obscure or non-existent, but which each instantiate a principle of mechanism (Snickars 2017). The science of mechanism was dubbed 'kinematics' by German engineer Franz Reuleaux, himself a source for Marx's study of capitalist machinery (Frison 1988: 303). It has since declined as a branch of engineering (Moon 2003).

9 'True, the annihilation of the I in the face of art is to be taken no more literally than is art ... aesthetic experiences are as such psychologically real, it would be impossible to understand them if they were simply part and parcel of the illusions of art. Experiences are not "as if". The disappearance of the I in the moment of the shudder is not real; but delirium, which has a similar aspect, is nevertheless incompatible with artistic experience. For a few moments the I becomes aware, in real terms, of the possibility of letting self-preservation fall away, though it does not actually succeed in realizing this possibility' (Adorno 2002: 245).

10 It is plausible to construe this activity as involving a 'technological monad', since in opening up and re-forming their identities on the basis of their technical activity, technological subjects also become independent reflections of the whole of social reality. Here, though, the relation is not past-oriented and critical but rests on a utopian decision about the future.

11 This relates to changes in habitus associated with technology use, such as learning to use a computer mouse when previously one had only ever used pen and paper. Such changes have implications for the symbolic mediation of personal identity – see Kirkpatrick (2015) for discussion of this in connection with computer gaming.

12 The defensive function of critique has a lineage stretching back to Kant, whose 1781 *Critique of Pure Reason* (1992) initiated the modern critical tradition by demonstrating the limits of scientific deduction as a method for addressing questions of a metaphysical nature. Kant placed his faith in a reason opposed to technical artifice when he argued that 'Men will of their own accord gradually work their way out of barbarism so long as artificial means are not deliberately adopted to keep them in' (1992: 59).

13 Feenberg argues that 'the substitution of "fast food" for the traditional family dinner can serve as a humble illustration of the unintended cultural consequences of technology' (2002: 7).

14 There is an interesting irony here in that while Srnicek and Williams (2017) and contemporary accelerationists are willing to imagine substantively different technologies, like spaceships for interstellar travel, they have nothing more than wishing to offer in relation to its reform, while Feenberg offers rich accounts of how technology has been shaped but only ever concerns himself with changes to its meaning, fighting shy of utopian recommendations concerning the technology of the future.

15 The software can be downloaded from: www.automation.strikenow.org.uk.

16 It seems to me that Universal Automation is not merely 'socially shaped' as part of a contest over meanings, but is better understood as technology that deliberately favours some ways of living, and even some people's interests, over others. Viewed in this way, it is less an intervention than an experiment in the development of infrastructure for a future society. To deliver on its utopian aspiration, the theory of technical politics needs to include the possibility of technology like this that is substantively biased by (progressive) design and has the capacity to force a new situation, every bit as much as the production-line imposed capitalist labour conditions onto generations of workers. The model here is not discursive but authoritative, even coercive, and the relevant value is not democracy but equality.

Beyond critique: utopia

My purpose in this book has been to show that Feenberg's intervention constitutes an important and much needed development of Marxian and critical theory in relation to technology. I have also argued that his work is a vital counterweight to other, non-critical tendencies in contemporary philosophy and sociology of technology, especially constructivism, ANT and post-phenomenology. In concluding, I will summarise the sense in which his work constitutes an advance and then review some of the suggestions I have made, in an effort to contribute to the further development of the theory.

As far as critical theory is concerned, Feenberg has continued and updated the tradition, retaining its focus on individual human self-realisation and the centrality of that idea to any meaningful conception of historical progress. Pursuant to this, his work takes as its problematic one of the most important questions of contemporary Marx scholarship, concerning the paradoxical relationship between technology and progressive social change. He is almost alone among Marx scholars of the past three or four decades in taking this question seriously and making it central to his attempt to reconstruct Marxist theory. That forms of social organisation and power familiar to people in capitalist societies also pervaded life in the Soviet Union and restricted its progress towards anything like socialism has been widely observed, but much of the theoretical reflection on this has involved genuflections to the role of 'technical reason' in domination, rather than investigating the concrete mediation of rationality and power that constitutes the technical. This evasion is somewhat of a travesty, and Feenberg's intervention must be seen as bringing some urgency to a question that has been deferred for far too long.

As part of this, Feenberg has also challenged the critical theory tradition's suspicion of technology, including the well-worn trope that technological rationality is integrally or essentially opposed to 'human' values of communication and meaning. Demonstrating that a humanist approach need not involve any such essentialism, Feenberg addresses this by incorporating social and historical factors into the definition of technology, and this is perhaps his most significant innovation. In this way, he has made it possible for critical theory to engage with technology as not merely a problem but also a locus of possibilities and potential. This move is also an important step towards clarification of the ways in which technology can become problematic for progressive politics, and has led to a corresponding sharpening of the analytical resources of critical theory. This is illustrated by the valuable concepts of technological ambivalence and progressive or democratic rationalisation, which are essential foundations for understanding technical politics.

None of the rival positions in contemporary critical theory have produced concepts with similar purchase on the technology–society relationship. Jürgen Habermas (2003) has written an interesting study of genetic medicine's potential to undermine the neuro-physical basis of democratic culture, but his basic model remains the dichotomy in which aspects of the technological system present a threat to the value basis of the cultural lifeworld. There is little sense in this work of the positive possibilities presented by genetic medicine. There are good reasons to be cautious, of course, when it comes to identifying political potential in the genetic modification of the unborn, but a theory that includes this opposition at its foundation seems likely always to be caught on the back foot when new technical capacities open up. Other contemporary critical theorists simply have nothing to say about technology. This becomes increasingly odd when so much of the empirical substance of society is technologically mediated. Critical theory's assumption that the fundamental processes are human-communicative, with technology only contemplated as some kind of historical accretion, feels increasingly out of touch in the age of social media.[1]

In contrast, Feenberg introjects social elements into the definition of technology. This undermines essentialism, while he retains many of its critical insights, and makes it possible to develop a richer, more nuanced conception of the entwinement of technological capabilities with human ones and their joint development through social and historical processes. The notion of technical politics as a site of struggle where these processes are mediated and subject to challenge is an important theoretical development. Understanding technical action in terms of political hegemony enables us to view the various interventions, hacktivisms and grass roots initiatives in terms of their wider significance.

Feenberg's work is also markedly superior to the depoliticised efforts that dominate in science and technology studies (STS). As we have seen, his embrace of constructivism enables him to develop ideas from critical theory in a new, productive conceptual space. Focusing on the processes through which social forces shape technological artefacts in development secures greatly enhanced relevance for critical social theory at a time when so much of life seems to involve these contests. Beyond this, though, drawing on ideas from contemporary political theory to develop the concept of technical politics, Feenberg has grasped the wider, political potential in such contests and articulated this to the reconstructed version of critical theory in his theory of progressive rationalisation. In place of catastrophism or implausible and unappealing doctrines of rupture, he offers a political theory of technical change that might be built upon in a practical sense, rather than leaving people hoping for divine intervention.

Having said all this in support of the idea of technical politics, though, a number of limitations must be acknowledged to the theory as currently formulated. First, technical politics is located in language, specifically in the processes through which technology is interpreted and its capabilities named, and we have seen in this book that the boundary between description and substantive reality is a repeated source of difficulty for the theory. Technology does not only exist as described but must be understood as involving objects that also act at the scene of design and elsewhere. A properly materialist philosophy of technology should be focused on opening up space in which objects may be heard. Retrieving the category of substantive bias, which Feenberg clarifies but then rejects, turns out to be a way to identify missing potential as well as identifying real evil in technologies of the past.

Secondly, the linkage from technical politics to civilisation change is fragile and requires some further support. Feenberg's conviction that more popular involvement in design will necessarily make for ethically superior technology – a conviction seemingly shared by Verbeek – is not obviously supported by the historical record. Similarly, the notion that more aesthetic technology designs, which play more easily on the senses and connect people and nature, will necessarily be less exploitative or susceptible to entanglements in strategies of domination must be approached with caution. The linkages between local interventions that alter specific devices and civilisation-defining shifts in the global meaning of 'technology' require further thought.

Finally, the rush to politicise, while justified with reference to the conservative apoliticism of much STS, runs the risk of obscuring a range of sociological questions. Feenberg follows STS into the analysis of situations and processes already defined as 'technical', and this is hazardous because many people, perhaps even the majority, do not get to play a shaping role or are restricted to marginal levels of participation. There is a sociology of access and exclusion that is largely left out of focus in the theory as it stands, and this is a particularly acute failing when technical politics is the only kind available. Critical theory of technology would benefit from engagement with a wider range of sociological theories to address this.

Having said this much, it is also surely the case that a dialogue with wider sociological theories would benefit them as much as it would Feenberg. In particular, recent sociological work on changes to the nature of labour and workplace organisations would benefit from engagement with constructivist ideas in a critical framework. In this book I have referred to Boltanski and Chiapello's important study of the 'new spirit of capitalism', which focuses on how the system has recuperated itself essentially by feigning to address the concerns of a generation of workers who refused to take up their roles in boring management and technical professions. The changes they describe were largely facilitated by technology that was shaped to the purpose, yet they completely overlook the issue. Similarly, Lazzaroto (2014) and Dardot and Laval (2014) have made arguments about the changing dynamics of subordination and domination in the workplace, which increasingly turn on subjects' internalisation of behavioural and other norms, accompanied by an ideology in which people are made to feel responsible for everything that happens to them. These important works neglect to discuss how digital technology has been moulded to facilitate and enforce these processes. The changes these authors describe have implications for the critical theory of technology, since capitalist technology extends its hold over people into deeper recesses of their inner lives and social relationships. At the same time, though, it must be noted that none of them have discussed the shaping of technology, especially digital technologies, to meet these new system requirements.

Peter-Paul Verbeek has criticised Feenberg's theory for lacking a properly ethical dimension specific to technology. It is true that Feenberg tends to view ethical criteria for technology as deriving from extra-technical discursive contexts. The problem with this approach comes into view when he seems to conflate better technology with more democratic involvement in design. Unfortunately, in contests over technology designs the fact that large numbers of people favour one option over another, or attribute some meanings to the exclusion of others, is not in itself sufficient to ensure that those designs are 'best'. It is entirely conceivable that large numbers of people, perhaps even a majority, operating within a democratic regulatory framework might choose unethical, even immoral technologies. Feenberg supposes that in a more democratic context, space will be created in which people can deliberate on the best course and that this will tend to result in more progressive designs. He suggests that superior designs will be those that are more attentive to the communicative aspect of technology, especially its symbolic integration into the wider life of the community. This preference, however, is not justified in any explicit account of design ethics.

Verbeek rightly suggests that what is needed is an ethics immanent to the technology design process, although this is something that he then fails to articulate in any detail. In contrast, Feenberg's theory of bias creates the theoretical conditions through which this idea might be advanced and, drawing on the rich heritage of critical theory, he did so well in advance of post-phenomenology's fashionable 'post-humanism'. Moreover, it is worth noting that for all his attempts to distance himself from Feenberg's approach, Verbeek only ends up joining him in calling for greater democracy in technology design.

Feenberg's theory includes resources to develop an immanent ethics of design because he identifies, in humanistic and pragmatic terms, the basic motivation of technology. His preferred example here is medicine, which he sometimes presents as paradigmatic for the positive technological employment of scientific knowledge (e.g. 2010: 81). For all that essentialists and others view technical action as marked by a kind of primal violence, Feenberg shows that this is intimately paralleled by a concern to make the world a better place. His dialectic of primary and secondary instrumentalisation includes this paradox at its very core, and its historical unfolding is what produces technology's ambivalence and the possibility of democratic rationalisation. His embrace of Marcuse's organicism leads Feenberg to frame the possibilities opened up by this theorisation in terms of a logic of reconciliation, according to which democratisation will restore technology to its original, beneficent social purposes.

I have tried to show that an Adornian position on this issue can sharpen the focus on an immanent ethics by focusing on identity and non-identity as this applies to technology itself. Presently, as technologists move to improve the world, so they instrumentalise it, themselves and, ultimately, everyone else as well, but they do so with at least some sense that they are contributing to progress. The prospect that, as Sartre put it, 'liberated society will be a harmonious enterprise of exploitation of the world' (1969: 224) seems fantastic now, but it is nonetheless conceivable that the benign motivations bound up in technological creativity might find themselves, if not emancipated, at least differently thwarted in a new social arrangement. If this sounds unpromising, it opens onto a technical politics that is not framed by the binary opposition of communication to instrumental domination, but rather presents multiple possibilities, each to be assessed through a *utopian*, future-facing calculation of their likely world impact. The ethics of democratic technical politics, then, start with a dialogue between people and things, with a renewed emphasis on responsibility as the basis of autonomy, rather than faith in the possibility of ultimate reconciliation. Utopianism here serves as a methodology for thinking the future, rather than a blueprint for utopia.

In this context, there is something to Bruno Latour's repudiation of critical theory from which Feenberg's theory might benefit. Latour identifies critique as a kind of impediment to thinking and acting differently, suggesting that it actually inhibits a different world-relation by tying subjectivity to a narrow conception of reality. For him, critical theorists are the 'ghouls' of social theory (2013b: 348), who are always equipped with explanations, normally of why things turned out so badly, but bereft of useful recommendations. His own suggestion is that theory should recognise that reality exceeds the 'truth' associated with various kinds of correspondence theory and elevated into disciplines positively associated with 'science'. That most people most of the time are not seeking scientific legitimacy for the beliefs with which they operate, and that these beliefs are nonetheless productive of determinate realities, ought to be experienced, he suggests, as liberating. The category-mistake checker that academic social scientists have been applying to their theories is itself a kind of category-mistake (Latour 2013b).

Latour presents this view as anti-critical because critical theory, which from its inception was concerned with setting limits to scientific reason, is one of the factors that prevents theory from simply strolling onto the ground he has identified – the social and cultural territory produced every day without reference to whether its operative statements are 'true'.[2] This is an interesting challenge to critical theory because it turns one of its own long-established arguments against it, namely the suggestion that reification is an illusion produced by those who are in thrall to it. Critical theory has often alleged that others are in the grip of a 'fear of freedom' or other kinds of false consciousness that lead them into conformist behaviours, which in turn reproduce a system that is not in their interests. Latour's argument is that by maintaining the dominant illusion that science and technology embody the only valid knowledge, critical theory is in fact complicit with its own mournful condition.

Socialist society will need its own technology and cannot rely upon passively inheriting what it needs from capitalism. Following through on this insight seems to require a type of thinking that is not compatible with 'critique'. Attachment to that figure of thought limits technical politics to the introjected binary of technology's 'ambivalence', while the objective situation contains more possibilities than can be addressed through a dialectical negation of capitalism's negation of technology's potential. A way of thinking the future that allows scope for what Adorno called 'exact fantasy'[3] seems to be necessary. I have suggested that Adorno's thought has something to offer theory that attempts to broach this question.

Latour's repudiation of critical theory reflects empirical changes of the last 40 years that concern the way that technology is experienced. I have argued in this book that Feenberg's notion that contemporary society is ruled by a technological hegemony, in which coercion is experienced as the imposition of technical norms, is at certain points out of step with this experience, which involves friendly gadgets and a technical infrastructure whose primary orientation is communicative, even playful. Technical politics must grasp the paradox of a technology that is no longer austere or brutal but remains implicated in domination, and relate this to its study of ongoing struggles over the meaning of technology.

The difficulty critical theory faces here is that the constellation has shifted, with the consequence that the mix of values and standards of what might be considered 'reasonable' demands on technology varies more widely than Feenberg's technical politics allows. Aesthetics, democracy and expertise are not easily assigned to 'sides' in an agonistic struggle against technical expertise over the shape or meaning of future technology. Moreover, while contests recognisable from the earlier period (over health, safety, etc.) have lost none of their importance, efficiency in design choices is rarely the central contested term in the way that it was before, because other values are now installed at the heart of technology design culture. Finally, the connection of technical politics to other struggles is not bridgeable via the notion of a 'hegemonic technological rationality' at work behind the scenes, forging a coherent web of domination that extends from the design of the latest phone to the opening hours of your local clinic.

It is curious that the main theoretical benefit from characterising technology as hegemonic should be an optimistic framing of popular technical activity that is unconstrained by hegemonic norms as 'resistance' or 'democratic technical politics', all adding up to a push towards a brighter future. From Latour's perspective, whether it adds up to anything is a matter to be determined by the activity itself, but in the absence of a ruling power there is no obstacle to inaugurating many new counts of the world, none of them aspiring to include everything that is in it. In his vision, however, the question of power remains unaddressed. Feenberg points to the entanglement of expert discourses with institutions closely allied to the state and to corporations. For most people, who are not internationally acclaimed university professors, stepping outside these constraints to promote alternative forms of knowing only invites various kinds of stigmatisation.

The political success of openly irrational movements in the past decade suggests that some kind of breach may have occurred in the knowledge–power nexus associated with modernity. Feenberg's theory of technical politics provides conceptual resources with which to understand the issues at stake in this new situation, as well as a strategic theorisation that clarifies its dangers and opportunities. He has succeeded in formulating a version of critical theory that speaks directly to twenty-first-century concerns.

Notes

1 This observation is not limited to critical theory but applies equally well to many areas of contemporary sociology, in which there has been a tendency towards 'micro' investigations (of 'art', 'music', even 'personal life') that purport to de-reify and explain their objects as emerging from strictly limited contexts. The absence of any reference to technologies in these studies is often indicative of their deceptive artificiality, or as Feenberg might put it, their abstract character.

2 Latour suggests 'felicitous' is a more useful term to describe the way statements perform their reality-producing functions.

3 "'Exact fantasy" was ... a dialectical concept which acknowledged the mutual mediation of subject and object without allowing either to get the upper hand' (Buck-Morss 1977: 86).

References

Adas, M. (1989) *Machines as the Measure of Men: Science, technology and ideologies of Western dominance*, Ithaca, NY: Cornell University Press.

Adorno, T.W. (2000) *Introduction to Sociology*, Stanford, CA: Stanford University Press.

Adorno, T.W. (2002) *Aesthetic Theory*, trans. R. Hullot-Kentor, London: Continuum.

Adorno, T.W. (2005) *Critical Models: Interventions and catchwords*, New York: Columbia University Press.

Adorno, T.W. and Horkheimer, M. (1997) *The Dialectic of Enlightenment*, trans. J. Hephcott, London: Verso.

Anderson, P. (2017) *The H-Word: The peripeteia of hegemony*, London: Verso.

Arnold, D. and Michel, A. (eds) (2017) *Critical Theory and the Thought of Andrew Feenberg*, Cham, Switzerland: Springer Nature.

Baber, Z. (1996) *The Science of Empire: Scientific knowledge, civilization and colonial rule in India*, New York: State University of New York Press.

Badiou, A. (2006) *Metapolitics*, London: Verso.

Bernal, M. (1987) *Black Athena: The Afro-Asiatic roots of ancient civilization*, New Brunswick, NJ: Rutgers University Press.

Bijker, W. (1997) *Of Bicycles, Bakelites, and Bulbs: Towards a theory of sociotechnical change*, London: MIT Press.

Bijker, W., Hughes, T. and Pinch, T. (1989) *On the Social Construction of Technological Systems*, London: MIT Press.

Boggs, C. (1976) *Gramsci's Marxism*, London: Pluto.

Boltanski, L. and Chiapello, E. (2005) *The New Spirit of Capitalism*, London: Verso.

Borgmann, A. (1984) *Technology and the Character of Contemporary Life: A philosophical inquiry*, London: University of Chicago Press.

Borgmann, A. (1999) *Holding onto Reality: The nature of information at the turn of the millennium*, Chicago: University of Chicago Press.

Bowker, G.C. and Star, S.L. (1999) *Sorting Things Out: Classification and its consequences*, London: MIT Press.

Braverman, H. (1974) *Labour and Monopoly Capital*, New York: Monthly Review Press.

Buck-Morss, S. (1977) *The Origin of Negative Dialectics: Theodor W. Adorno, Walter Benjamin and the Frankfurt Institute*, New York: The Free Press.

Canguilheim, G. (2007) *The Normal and the Pathological*, New York: Urzone, Inc.

Chabot, P. (2013) *The Philosophy of Simondon*, London: Bloomsbury.

Chandler, A. (1996) 'The changing definition and image of hackers in popular discourse', in *International Journal of the Sociology of Law* 24.

Cockburn, C. (1983) *Brothers: Male dominance and technological change*, London: Pluto Press.

Cohen, G.A. (1978) *Karl Marx's Theory of History: A defence*, Oxford: Clarendon Press.

Claeys, G. (2018) *An Introduction to Marx and Marxism*, Harmondsworth: Penguin.

Dardot, P. and Laval, P. (2014) *The New Way of the World: On neo-liberal society*, London: Verso.

De Certeau, M. (1984) *The Practice of Everyday Life*, Berkeley: University of California Press.

De Vries, M.J. (ed.) (2015) 'Book symposium on the philosophy of Simondon: Between technology and individuation', in *Philosophy & Technology* 28(2).

Ellul, J. (1964) *The Technological Society*, New York: Knopf.

Elster, J. (1986) *Making Sense of Marx*, Cambridge: Cambridge University Press.

Eribon, D. (2011) *Michel Foucault*, Paris: Flammarion Champs Biographie.

Feenberg, A. (1981) *Lukacs, Marx and the Sources of Critical Theory*, Oxford: Oxford University Press.

Feenberg, A. (1991) *Critical Theory of Technology*, Oxford: Oxford University Press.

Feenberg, A. (1992) 'Subversive rationality: Technology, power and democracy', in *Inquiry: An Interdisciplinary Journal of Philosophy* 35(3–4).

Feenberg, A. (1995) *Alternative Modernity: The technical turn in philosophy and social theory*, Berkeley: University of California Press.

Feenberg, A. (2001) *Questioning Technology*, London: Routledge.

Feenberg, A. (2002) *Transforming Technology: A critical theory revisited*, Oxford: Oxford University Press.

Feenberg, A. (2003) 'Democratic rationalization: Technology, power and freedom', in Scharff, R. and Dusek, V. (eds) *Philosophy of Technology: The technological condition*, Oxford: Blackwell.

Feenberg, A. (2005) *Heidegger and Marcuse: The catastrophe and redemption of history*, London: Routledge.

Feenberg, A. (2008) 'Marcuse on art and technology', paper presented to Radical Philosophy Association Conference, www.researchgate.net/publication/242512716_Marcuse_on_Art_and_Technology. Accessed 2 January 2019.

Feenberg, A. (2010) *Between Reason and Experience: Essays in technology and modernity*, London: MIT Press.

Feenberg, A. (2017) *Technosystem: The social life of reason*, Cambridge, MA: Harvard University Press.

Feenberg, A. and Freedman, J. (2001) *When Poetry Ruled the Streets: the French May events of 1968*, New York: SUNY Press.

Foster, H. (2002) *Design and Crime (and Other Diatribes)*, London: Verso.

Foucault, M. (1981) 'The order of discourse', in Young, R. (ed.) *Untying the Text: A post-structuralist reader*, London: RKP.

Foucault, M. (1985) *Madness and Civilization: A history of insanity in the age of reason*, London: Random House.

Foucault, M. (1986) *The Birth of the Clinic*, trans. A.M. Sheridan, London: Routledge.

Foucault, M. (2005) *The Hermeneutics of the Subject: Lectures at the Collège de France 1981–2*, Basingstoke: Palgrave Macmillan.

Freiberger, P. and Swaine, M. (1984) *Fire in the Valley: The making of the personal computer*, London: McGraw-Hill.

Frison, M. (1988) 'Technical and technological innovation in Marx', in *History and Technology* 6.

Geras, N. (1987) 'Post-Marxism', in *New Left Review* 163.

Goggin, G. and Newell, C. (2003) *Digital Disability*, Melbourne: Hodder and Stoughton.

Goldmann, L. (1977) *Lukàcs and Heidegger: Towards a new philosophy*, trans. W.Q. Boelhower, London: Routledge Kegan Paul.

Gomart, E. and Hennion. A. (1999) 'A sociology of attachment: Music lovers, drug users', in Law, J. and Hassard, J. (eds) *ANT and after*, Oxford: Oxford University Press.

Gramsci, A. (1982) *Prison Notebooks*, London: Lawrence & Wishart.

Greenfield, A. (2018) 'China's dystopian tech could be contagious', in *The Atlantic*, 14 February, www.theatlantic.com/technology/archive/2018/02/chinas-dangerous-dream-of-urban-control/553097. Accessed 14 February 2019.

Habermas, J. (1985) *The Theory of Communicative Action Volume 2: Lifeworld and system, a critique of functionalist reason*, Cambridge: Polity.

Habermas, J. (1989) *Towards a Rational Society*, trans. J.J. Shapiro, Cambridge: Polity.

Habermas, J. (1990) *Moral Consciousness and Communicative Action*, Cambridge: Polity.

Habermas, J. (1992) *Post-Metaphysical Thinking*, Cambridge: Polity.

Habermas, J. (2003) *The Future of Human Nature*, Cambridge: Polity.

Hacking, I. (1999) *The Social Construction of What?* London: Harvard University Press.

Hamer, E. (2005) *Adorno and the Political*, London: Routledge.

Han, B. (1998) *Foucault's Critical Project*, Stanford, CA: Stanford University Press.

Hansen, A.D. (2014) 'Laclau and Mouffe and the ontology of radical negativity', in *Distinktion* 15(3).

Haraway, D. (1991) *Simians, Cyborgs and Women: The reinvention of nature*, London: Routledge.

Harvey, D. (2010) *A Companion to Marx's Capital*, London: Verso.

Hayles, N.K. (1999) *How We Became Post-Human: Virtual bodies in cybernetics, literature and informatics*, Chicago: University of Chicago Press.

Heidegger, M. (1987) *Being and Time*, trans. J. MacQuarrie and E. Robertson, Oxford: Blackwell.

Heidegger, M. (2013) *The Question Concerning Technology and Other Essays*, New York: Harper Perennial.

Heidegger, M. (2014) *Poetry, Language, Thought*, New York: Harper Perennial.

Hennion, A. (1995) 'The history of art', in *Réseaux* 3.

Hughes, T. (ed.) (1983) *Social Construction of Technical Systems*, Cambridge, MA: MIT Press.

Hullot-Kentor, R. (2006) *Things beyond Resemblance: Collected essays from Theodor Adorno*, New York: Columbia University Press.

Jäger, L. (2004) *Adorno: A political biography*, New Haven, CT, and London: Yale University Press.

Jennings, H. (1985) *Pandaemonium: The coming of the machine as seen by contemporary observers*, Basingstoke: Palgrave.

Kant, I. (1992) *Political Writings*, trans. and ed. H. Reiss, Cambridge: Cambridge University Press.

Khatchatourov, A. (ed.) (2019) *Les identités numeriques en tension*, Paris: ISTE Editions.

Kirkpatrick, G. (2004/2017) *Critical Technology: A social theory of personal computing*, London: Ashgate.

Kirkpatrick, G. (2013) *Computer Games and the Social Imaginary*, Cambridge: Polity.

Kirkpatrick, G. (2015) 'Ludefaction: Fracking of the radical imaginary', in *Games & Culture* 10(6).

Korsch, K. (1970) *Marxism and Philosophy*, New York: Modern Reader Books.

Laclau, E. (1979) *Politics and Ideology in Marxist Theory*, London: Verso.

Laclau, E. and Mouffe, C. (1985) *Hegemony and Socialist Strategy: Towards a radical democratic politics*, London: Verso.

Latour, B. (1993) *We Have Never Been Modern*, Cambridge, MA: Harvard University Press.

Latour, B. (2005) *Reassembling the Social: An introduction to actor-network-theory*, Oxford: Oxford University Press.

Latour, B. (2013a) *Rejoicing: Or the torments of religious speech*, Cambridge: Cambridge University Press.

Latour, B. (2013b) *An Inquiry into Modes of Existence: An anthropology of the moderns*, trans. C. Porter, New York: Harvard University Press.

Law, J. and Hassard, J. (eds) (2006) *ANT and after*, Oxford: Oxford University Press.

Lazzaroto, M. (2014) *Signs and Machines*, London: Semiotext(e).

Leskanich, A. (2017) 'Book review: Facing Gaia: Eight lectures on the new climatic regime by Bruno Latour', at http://blogs.lse.ac.uk/lsereviewofbooks/2017/08/24/book-review-facing-gaia-eight-lectures-on-the-new-climatic-regime-by-bruno-latour. Accessed 14 February 2019.

Levy, S. (1984) *Hackers: Heroes of the computer revolution*, Harmondsworth: Penguin.

Lukàcs, G. (1981) *History and Class Consciousness*, London: Merlin Press.

Macpherson, C.B. (1962) *The Political Theory of Possessive Individualism: Hobbes to Locke*, Oxford: Clarendon Press.

McNay, L. (2014) *The Misguided Search for the Political*, Cambridge: Polity.

Marcuse, H. (1961) *Eros and Civilization*, New York: Beacon Press.

Marcuse, H. (1964) *One-Dimensional Man*, London: RKP.

Marcuse, H. (1978) *The Aesthetic Dimension*, London: Macmillan.

Marx, K. (1970) *A Contribution to the Critique of Political Economy*, Moscow: Progress.

Marx, K. (1978) *Critique of the Gotha Programme*, Moscow: Progress.

Marx, K. (1981) *Grundrisse*, trans. M. Nicolaus, Harmondsworth: Penguin.

Marx, K. (1983) *Economic and Philosophical Manuscripts of 1844*, London: Lawrence & Wishart.

Marx, K. (1990) *Capital: A critique of political economy*, trans. B. Fowkes, London: Penguin.

Marx, K. and Engels, F. (1958) *Selected Works* (2 vols), Moscow: Progress.

Marx, K. and Engels, F. (1967) *The Communist Manifesto*, Harmondsworth: Penguin.

Marx, K. and Engels, F. (1982) *The German Ideology*, ed. and introduction C.J. Arthur, London: Lawrence & Wishart.

Misa, T.J. Brey, P. and Feenberg, A. (2003) *Modernity and Technology*, London: MIT Press.

Moon, F.C. (2003) 'Franz Releau: Contributions to 19th century kinematics and theory of machines', in *Applied Mechanics Review* 56(2).

Negroponte, N. (1999) *Being Digital*, London: Coronet.

Neville, R. (1971) *Playpower*, London: Paladin.

O'Connor, B. (2012) *Adorno*, London: Routledge.

Popper, K. (1989) *Conjectures and Refutations*, London: Routledge.

Rancière, J. (2009) *The Emancipated Spectator*, London: Verso.

Reiner, R. (2000) *The Politics of the Police*, Oxford: Oxford University Press.

Sartre, J.-P. (1969) *Literary and Philosophical Essays*, London: Hutchinson.

Scharff, R.C. and Dusek, V. (eds) (2003) *Philosophy of Technology: The technological condition*, Oxford: Blackwell.

Snickars, P. (2017) 'Metamodelling – 3D-scanning Christopher Polhem's Laboratorium Mechanicum', http://pellesnickars.se/2017/01/metamodeling-polhem. Accessed February 2019.

Srnicek, N. and Williams, A. (2017) *Inventing the Future: Postcapitalism and a world without work*, London: Verso.

Stedman-Jones, G. (2016) *Karl Marx: Greatness and illusion*, Harmondsworth: Penguin.

Turkle, S. (1995) *Life on the Screen*, New York: Simon & Schuster.

Turner, F. (2006) *From Counter-Culture to Cyber-Culture*, Chicago: Chicago University Press.

Veak, T. (ed.) (2006) *Democratising Technology: Andrew Feenberg's critical theory of technology*, New York: SUNY Press.

Verbeek, P.-P. (2006) *What Things Do: Philosophical reflections on technology, agency, and design*, University Park, PA: Penn State Press.

Verbeek, P.-P. (2013) 'Resistance is futile: Towards a non-modern democratization of technology' in *Techné: Research in Philosophy and Technology* 17(1).

Wacjman, J. (2004) *Technofeminism*, Cambridge: Polity.

Weber, M. (1974) *The Protestant Ethic and the Rise of Capitalism*, London: Routledge Kegan Paul.

Winner, L. (1993) 'Upon opening the black box and finding it empty: Social constructivism and the philosophy of technology', *Science, Technology & Human Values* 18(3).

Witkin, R. (1998) *Adorno on Music*, London: Routledge.

Wood, A. (2004) *Karl Marx*, London: Routledge.

Index

accelerationism 2, 147n.14
Adorno, T.W. 5, 22, 32, 42, 44n.13, 50,
   67n.3, 106–108, 121n.20, 137
aesthetics 4, 7, 31, 92, 123, 129, 138,
   143, 146n.9, 150, 154
  aesthetic index 11, 106
  aesthetic values 42–43, 66, 111,
    114–119
  normative 102, 105, 120n.9, 136
  (re-)aestheticisation 18, 34, 73,
    96–98, 104, 111–116,
    121n.17, 137
  superimposition 116–117
  see also modernism
ambivalence 2, 14, 32–36, 109, 133,
   149, 152, 153
Anderson, P. 93
anti-technology 8, 53, 98
authenticity 8, 44, 71, 106, 117, 119,
   126, 138, 144
authority 25, 28, 36, 39, 41, 76, 142
autonomy *see* operational autonomy

Baber, Z. 64
Badiou, A. 4, 9
Bernal, M. 64
bias 11, 14, 43, 46, 51, 64, 67n.5, 70,
   133, 147, 150
  constitutive/implementation 47,
    55–56
  formal 15, 47–48, 52–59, 63, 66,
    68n.9, 71, 79, 91, 133
  progressive substantive 67n.5,
    124, 142

substantive 15–16, 47, 52, 56,
   59–63, 66, 100
bicycles 23, 37, 76, 119n.1
Bijker, W. 94n.10
blind, visually impaired 58
Boggs, C. 93
boilers 38–39, 82
  see also efficiency, contested
   definition
Boltanski, L. 65–66, 69n.20, 114, 151
Borgmann, A. 52
Brand, R. 8

Canguilheim, G. 45n.20
capitalism 65–66, 83, 110, 136, 143
  distorting technology 15, 52–54, 58,
   111, 123, 135, 153
  historical development 13, 24,
   43n.3, 99
  informational 65–66, 114, 116,
   121n.21, 151
  and societal rationalisation 28,
   50–51
  see also Weber, M.
Chiapello, E. 65–66, 69n.20, 114, 151
civilisational change 33–35, 87, 92, 97,
   102, 111, 143
  see also utopia
Claeys, G. 42, 44n.16
Cockburn, C. 58, 59, 60
codification *see* technical code
Cohen, G. A. 42
collector (Latour) 84
communication 6–8, 114, 140–143, 149